STANLEY SPENCER'S GREAT WAR DIARY: 1915–1918

A Personal Account of Active Service on the Western Front

STANLEY SPENCER'S GREAT WAR DIARY: 1915–1918

by

Stanley Spencer

Edited by Tony Spencer

Pen & Sword
MILITARY

First published in Great Britain in 2008
and republished in this format in 2022 by
Pen & Sword Military
an imprint of
Pen & Sword Books Ltd
Yorkshire – Philadelphia

ISBN 978 1 39907 462 9

Typeset in Sabon by Phoenix Typesetting
Printed and bound in the UK by CPI Group (UK) Ltd, Croydon, CR0 4YY

Pen & Sword Books Limited incorporates the imprints of Atlas, Archaeology,
Aviation, Discovery, Family History, Fiction, History, Maritime, Military,
Military Classics, Politics, Select, Transport, True Crime, Air World,
Frontline Publishing, Leo Cooper, Remember When, Seaforth Publishing, The
Praetorian Press, Wharncliffe Local History, Wharncliffe Transport,
Wharncliffe True Crime, White Owl and After the Battle.

For a complete list of Pen & Sword titles please contact

PEN & SWORD BOOKS LIMITED
47 Church Street, Barnsley, South Yorkshire, S70 2AS, England
E-mail: enquiries@pen-and-sword.co.uk
Website: www.pen-and-sword.co.uk

or

PEN AND SWORD BOOKS
1950 Lawrence Rd, Havertown, PA 19083, USA
E-mail: Uspen-and-sword@casematepublishers.com
Website: www.penandswordbooks.com

Contents

Foreword

My father, Charles William Stanley Spencer, was born in Sheffield on 2 July 1890.

He was the only son of Louis Spencer, a Sheffield bank manager. As a young man he also worked in the bank before volunteering for army service.

Stanley Spencer enlisted as a private in the Royal Fusiliers in 1915, was commissioned in 1917 and served with the West Yorkshire Regiment until being demobilized early in 1919. He saw active service on the Western Front from 1915 until 1918 and the end of the Great War, 'the war to end wars'. He was slightly wounded on three occasions and was awarded the Military Cross for his leading part in a successful trench raid on 1 August 1918.

'Babs' Ramsden (H. Warwick Ramsden from Leeds) was his friend from 1917 and served with him in the West Yorkshire Regiment in France. After the war he was best man at my father's wedding to my mother, Molly Breakey, on 3 July 1924, and subsequently became my godfather.

Not long afterwards my father fell ill and was an invalid for the rest of his life.

He suffered from tuberculosis of both kidneys and died on 7 July 1943, aged fifty-three.

John Anthony Spencer

Abbreviations

AA	anti-aircraft
BEF	British Expeditionary Force
CCS	Casualty Clearing Station
CO	Commanding Officer
Coy	Company
CSM	Company Sergeant Major
DSO	Distinguished Service Order
GOC	General Officer Commanding
GS	General Service
GSO	General Staff Officer
HE	high explosive
HLI	Highland Light Infantry
HQ	headquarters
HVic	high velocity
IO	Intelligence Officer
MC	Military Cross
MG	machine-gun
MM	Military Medal
OC	Officer Commanding
OP	observation post
PMC	President of the Mess Committee
PT	physical training
RAMC	Royal Army Medical Corps
RE	Royal Engineers
RF	Royal Fusiliers
RFC	Royal Flying Corps
RTO	Railway Transport Officer
SAA	small arms ammunition
YZ	the day before an attack
Z	the day of an attack (zero)

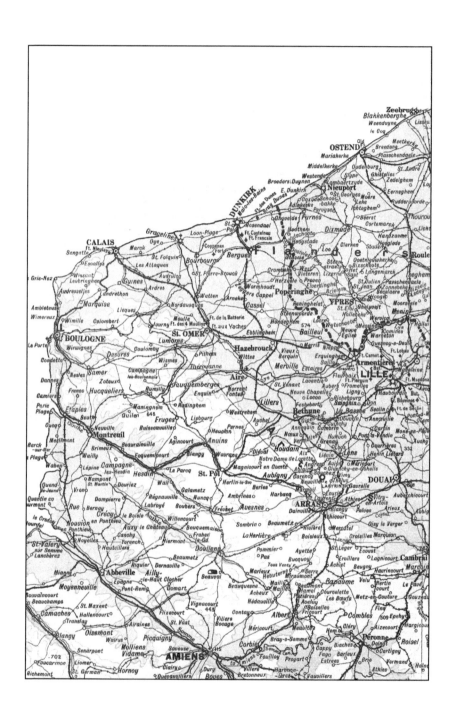

1915

January

I enlisted in the 24th (Service) Battalion of the Royal Fusiliers (known as the 2nd Sportsmen's Battalion) on 14 January. I was a private in 13 Platoon, D Company, and we trained in England for most of the year.

From January until 17 March our Headquarters were the Hotel Cecil, Strand, London, but then we moved to our new camp at Gidea Park, Romford, Essex. We paraded on the Guards' Square behind Whitehall on that day, marched through the City of London, passed the Mansion House where the Lord Mayor of London in full robes watched us go past, and entrained at Liverpool Street Station for Romford. We remained there until 26 June when we moved to Clipstone Camp near Mansfield. On 4 August we left Clipstone and went to Candahar Barracks, Tidworth, on Salisbury Plain, where we stayed until ordered overseas in November.

November

Our Battalion was in 99 Brigade, 33rd Division, and on 8 November a grand review and march past of the whole Division, with transport, was held on Salisbury Plain. The

King was to have been present but as he had recently suffered a serious accident, the Queen and Princess Mary came instead.

On the morning of 15 November we marched out from Candahar Barracks for the last time and entrained for Southampton which we reached at about 1.00 pm. We heard that because there were enemy submarines in the Channel we would not be able to leave port until after dark, so we remained sitting about on the platform until 5.30 pm when we went on board. The transport was the *Mona's Queen*, built in 1885 for the Isle of Man service. She had been painted black when requisitioned for trooping in March 1915. We were issued with lifebelts and went below at once. We were very crowded and I lay on the wood floor most of the night and by so doing probably escaped seasickness. At about 3.00 am we ran into the estuary at Le Havre and disembarked at 7.30 am. It was cold and bleak as we lined up on the quay and as we marched through the town and on to the 'Rest Camp' it began to snow heavily.

The Rest Camp itself consisted of a great number of Army bell tents in rows in a large field and the whole place was a sea of mud. There were no plank walks or even cinder tracks between the rows of tents and it was impossible to go a dozen yards without being ankle deep in squelching mud and pools of water. Fortunately the bell tents had the usual wooden floorboards and a little drain dug round each one, but as there were thirteen of us to each tent, and as each man's boots were smothered in mud as he walked in, it was not long before the tent floor became unsuitable to sleep on. We were issued with two blankets each and before nightfall collected some bits of stick with which to scrape our boots as we came into the tent. Early in the evening we set about the business of settling down as well as we could for the night. We laid our mackintosh sheets on the dirty floor, put all our equipment and our boots round the edge of the boards, stacked our rifles against the pole in the centre and all lay down with our feet to the middle. It snowed during the night and the tent leaked water onto several of us, but we were tired and used to hard beds so slept pretty well.

I woke up in the early morning stiff, cold and more or less damp, but reveille sounded soon after and we all got up, put on our boots and puttees (which were all we had taken off the night before) and splashed across the mud to the 'wash house'. This was a long corrugated-iron shed with a wide wooden bench down the middle. Cold water was laid on from taps at intervals along the bench and soap provided. Here we washed and shaved as well as we could. Light was admitted into the shed by the simple expedient of having no corrugated sheeting on the framework between the roof and the crossbar which was about four feet from the ground. This allowed the icy wind to blow straight through the place. Breakfast was served in a marquee. We all lined up at the entrance and were handed battered enamelled mugs containing a brown liquid referred to as 'tea' together with a hunk of bread and a rasher of bacon. We heard that we could get leave from the Rest Camp to go into the town from 10.30 am to 4.00 pm, so most of us went. I went with Scott, the signaller, and Hicks (Cupid). We wandered round Le Havre and had a good lunch and tea. After returning to the camp we had supper of bread and butter and cocoa before turning into our tents.

The next morning (the 18th) reveille was at 4.00 am and after an early breakfast we marched off to the station en route for the front. The train consisted of a series of carriages for the officers and cattle trucks for the men. There were thirty-nine men in my cattle truck! We moved out of Le Havre station at 10.30 am and spent 17½ hours in that truck. It was only heated by the bodies of the men themselves and we were too crowded to lie down on the floor properly. I spent the whole time either standing or sitting on my pack. We had a hurricane lamp lit during the night, and rumbled and chattered along hour after hour until at last at

8.00am on the 19th we reached Thiennes where we detrained. When we started on this long and miserably uncomfortable journey we each had a day's rations of bread, Army biscuits, bully beef and water, and in the afternoon we stopped somewhere and had hot tea brought round the trucks. We did not know where we were going and had no idea that we should be anything like that length of time on the way. Morning became afternoon and it gradually grew dark; then hour after hour slowly dragged by through the night and we became more and more tired, cramped, wretchedly uncomfortable and generally 'fed up'.

We had brought with us from England one blanket each in addition to our mackintosh sheet and full marching order, and the blanket was strapped on the top of the valise (or pack). We were therefore pretty well weighed down that morning for our 4-mile march from the station at Thiennes to Steenbecque village. It was a terribly long 4 miles but we got there and our section was billeted in a hay loft over a stable. It was quite dark in the loft, but we crawled in amongst the hay and slept like logs for hours. Later on we noticed an unpleasant smell in this loft – where we were billeted for three nights – and discovered that it was due to the presence down below of three cows, two pigs and a WC! This last was of the normal French type, without any drains. For the next two days we had the usual parades and a march to Hazebrouck and back. In the evenings we went to a farm-house nearby for coffees which were always served in small basins without handles. I never saw a cup with a handle in a French cottage or farm. I ran short of money here and wrote home for some, borrowing about 2/- * for more coffees from Green in the meantime.

On the morning of 22 November we left Steenbecque and marched to Busnes. The roads were bad and we found the

---

* Two shillings (10p)

French pavé particularly wearying. We were now carrying a
very full kit, much more than we had been accustomed to in
England, and the strain on our shoulders and ankles was
very great. It was about 13 miles to Busnes and many men
fell out before we got there. We were billeted in another hay
loft at Busnes. In the morning we found all the water frozen
and I shaved in the farmyard in some tepid tea in my mess
tin. We were to remain at Busnes that day and I was
detailed for twenty-four hours' Battalion Guard. The 'guard
room' was a hen pen near the transport lines! It was very
cold as two sides were only wire netting. During the night
we were supposed to see that the horses were quiet and did
not stray. We had a rather lively time because two of them
broke loose and galloped off round the fields. We could
hear them charging about in the mud but a rifle and fixed
bayonet are not much use in attempting to catch loose
horses and the transport men had to collect them in the
morning.

We moved again on the 24th and as we were still the
Battalion Guard we had to march with fixed bayonets. We
arrived at Fouquereuil in the afternoon and were relieved by
a fresh guard at about 4.00 pm. Our section's billet at
Fouquereuil was a much damaged house with a very leaky
roof. We were in one of the upstairs rooms and water
dripped steadily through the ceiling onto the half-rotten
floor. The glass had long since gone from the windows so we
had plenty of fresh air. On the 26th it snowed again and was
extremely cold. In the afternoon we got leave to go into
Béthune which was about two and a half miles away. I did
not think a great deal of Béthune; no doubt it looked better
in summer and in peacetime. The roads outside the town
were very bad and deep in mud; those in the town were all
of very badly laid stone sets. The shops were small and most
of the streets very narrow. We got back to our billet after
dark and then went to a cottage for chip potatoes, wine
and coffee. On the 27th we had our first pay day in France

and I received five francs! On the 28th we had reveille at 3.00 am and at 5.30 am we left for Annequin on the main road between Béthune and La Bassée.

On the 30th two notable events occurred. I received my first letter from home enclosing £2.00 in gold for which I was very thankful, and we went up into the communication trenches for the first time for which I was not so thankful. We went up the La Bassée road, turned to the left at 'Cambrin Fort' along 'Harley Street' which was really part of Cuinchy, and then turned to the right just short of the 'Pont Fixe', through the yard and round the huge shell holes at the big ruined brewery or iron works there – I forget which it had been – and so reached the entrance to the communication trench that ran up to the front line. This trench had no revetment or floorboards but was paved with bricks. And it was two to three feet deep in water at the time, so it was not long before we were soaked to the knees and covered in mud from head to foot. We had the useless old-fashioned French type of shovels with long handles and we threw more mud and water over ourselves than we did out of the trench. Occasional rifle and machine-gun bullets 'pinged' overhead, but the trench was very deep and we were really quite safe from them. There was no shelling there that night.

December

A few days previous to this I had volunteered for a bombing course and on 1 December I went to Beuvry for the first of three days' bombing instruction. There was a Brigade Bombing School just outside the village and we threw various types of bombs from a series of model trenches. We had some excitement one day when a man who was taking the course threw a live bomb which hit the top of the parapet and fell back into the trench. The man and the Bombing

Officer and sergeant dashed round the traverse just in time before it exploded. On 4 December the course was over and on the same day the Battalion moved from Annequin to Le Preôl where we were billeted in the attic of a fairly large house. We got up and down by step ladders as there were no stairs.

On the night of 6 December we went into the front line for the first time. We left Le Preôl at 2.15 pm and marched up to 'Harley Street' where we were met by guides from the 2nd Highland Light Infantry who we were going to relieve. It was raining hard and we had to wait in Harley Street for some time until it was dark enough to go forward as the HLI reported that the trenches were flooded and impassable so that we should have to reach the front line over the top. Just after dusk we started off – wet and cold to begin with – and slithered and slid and stumbled over the shell-torn, corpse-strewn wilderness known as the 'Valley of Death', where the English Guards had met and defeated the Prussian Guards many months before.

It was still raining and soon became inky dark and impossible to see even the ground under our feet except when a star shell went up. Weighed down as we were in full marching order we slipped and fell, caked ourselves with mud, paused for a few seconds quite still as a star shell lit up the waste of mud and then scrambled after the vanishing figure of the next man in front as the column moved on once more. Once Billy Haigh dropped on hands and knees in the slime and as a light went up found he had put his hand into the decomposing face of one of the enemy dead.

On our way over the top we had to cross over several communication and other trenches, and planks had been thrown across them for that purpose. Owing to the extreme darkness and also to the temporary blindness induced by the occasional vivid star shells, it was difficult to see exactly where they were or whether any trench was being crossed at all. When we were a short distance from the front line I walked off the edge of one of these planks before I realized that a trench was there below and I fell with a splash a distance of about seven feet into the mud and water at the bottom. A light went up as I slipped and I well remember seeing the black sides of the trench apparently shoot upwards before I landed on my back in the thick mud. I had some difficulty in regaining my feet as my heavy pack was stuck in the slime and when I did get up I had to grope about under the water for my rifle which I had dropped in the fall. The platoon was moving on without knowing of my sudden disappearance, but fortunately for me Green, who was one of the last men, saw me trying to scramble up the sticky sides and grabbed one end of my rifle and helped to haul me out. I was caked thick with mud and soaked with water. When we got into the front line and packs were taken off, one of the fellows had to help me to find the buckles at the back of mine before I could get it undone.

A few men of the HLI had been left in the trenches to give us an idea of how to carry on as this was our first time up. I spent the night partly standing on the slippery sandbags of the fire step, partly digging mud from the bottom of the trench and partly helping to remake the parapet a little farther along where it had been blown in by a shell. As it gradually became light in the early morning we had a better idea of our immediate surroundings. The trench was about nine feet deep without revetment or flooring. The mud at the bottom was very thick and it was impossible to walk about in the ordinary way as we sank in a foot or eighteen inches at every step and had the greatest difficulty in dragging our boots out again. During the night we had attempted to dig some out with spades but it clung fast and it was impossible to throw it clear. We soon gave up that method in favour of picking up huge handfuls and slinging it over the parados like that. The result of this was that about a week later all my fingernails dropped off and it was several weeks before new ones grew and got hard again.

We could not see beyond the traverse of our fire bay on the right-hand side, but on the left the ground fell away somewhat and we could see where the firing line ran over a slight ridge about 200 yards distant. One word summed up the view – mud. Everyone was deep in it, everything was thick with it, the trenches were half full of it and the whole district seemed made of it. During the night I was cold and in the morning I became hungry. Some bread and a pot of jam arrived from somewhere and we were about to have 'breakfast' in our fire bay when the enemy began to shell the front line on the little ridge to our left and the lower ground rather nearer. This was our first experience of anything beyond an occasional long-range shell or two while we were in reserve billets round Annequin and Beuvry. Most of the men gave up the idea of breakfast as little shell splinters came hissing round, but I was too 'fed up' by then to worry about such trifles and went steadily on with my bread and jam while the going was good. During the night there had been a fair amount of sniping and by the light of the star shells we could see two little wooden crosses out in 'No Man's Land' which had been put up by enemy snipers to show where they had shot our men out on patrol. During the day there was little to do except watch the front as well as possible with the aid of little pocket 'periscope' mirrors clipped on to bayonets held above the parapet.

At five o'clock that afternoon we were relieved by the Worcesters and began to move out. It was dusk when we started and on account of the flooded condition of the trenches it was decided we should go out by way of the towpath of the La Bassée Canal which ran through our lines and back to Béthune. It was very necessary to make no noise as the towpath was directly exposed to enemy fire from further up the canal towards La Bassée, so we crept stealthily out of the trench and down a muddy bank on to the towpath and underneath a large bridge that spanned the canal. It was a tiring march along the muddy path in the dark with the water of the canal gleaming a foot or two on our right and occasional little streams or dykes to jump across blindly, but after about 2 miles we were clear of the trench system and came out onto a road. The whole of this way we were under occasional machine-gun fire from further up the canal but fortunately no one was hit.

It was difficult in the dark to distinguish the path from the rushes that grew in the water close to the bank and one of our platoon, little Wright, fell into the canal and was rescued with difficulty from drowning by the HLI officer who was guiding us out. When we reached the road our guides left us to make the rest of our way back to the billets at Le Preôl, but it was not long before we reached a fork which was not recognized by our officers and no one knew which road we should take. Somebody went to enquire while we waited at the fork but we were all so completely tired out that every one of us, careless of the muddy road, lay down full length to rest just where we stood – and many of us immediately fell sound asleep – until the right road was decided upon and we wearily and miserably scrambled to our feet again, and trailed back to our bare, hard-boarded attic at Le Preôl. During the latter part of the march it rained steadily and when we reached our billets at 10.00 pm we were soaked with rain and plastered with trench mud from head to foot. None of us had had any sleep the previous night in the front line and everyone was dead beat. Nevertheless I stayed up until 1.15 am getting my rifle thoroughly clean again and then, as we had no fires and it was impossible to dry any clothes, I simply took off my mud-caked puttees and boots, rolled myself up in my blankets and slept like a log with my soaking clothes gradually drying on me.

We had certainly hoped for a day's rest in our billets after this first experience but we were disappointed. At 6.00 am (after I had had about four and a half hours' sleep) reveille sounded and we got up, had breakfast, scraped the thickest of the mud from our boots and puttees and 'fell in' for the trenches again at 7.45 am. We started off in the driving rain, stiff and tired at the very commencement, carrying our full marching order as before, and at length reached a part of the support line in the 'Brickfields' area at 12 noon. We relieved our own B Company there. The trench was not revetted (i.e. the trench sides were not supported by wood frames or walls of sandbags or in any other way) and it was not long before the sides began to fall in here and there under the influence of the continuous rain, filling the trench bottom with heaps of earth that were soon churned up into slimy mud, and raising the level of the water that was already several inches deep when we arrived.

As the afternoon passed and it grew dark the conditions got steadily worse. The trench sides continued to fall in, the water got deeper and deeper and it looked as though we were going to be drowned out. It was said that the enemy on the higher ground were pumping water out of their trenches and down the slope into ours. It continued to rain heavily all through the night. Billy Haigh had taken off his greatcoat while digging mud out of the trench bottom and afterwards could not find it in the dark. It was not until hours afterwards that someone digging under the water and into the bottom slime felt something spongy and difficult to move that proved to be the missing coat – in a perfectly indescribable condition, of course. When dragged out it was an enormous weight on account of the water it held and when we were relieved the next day he was obliged finally to abandon it in order to have sufficient strength to get out himself.

There was a sheet of corrugated iron over the bit of the trench we were in and during the first part of the night four of us crowded under it out of the rain, three sitting on the firing step and I on a burnt-out brazier, all of us nearly up to the knees in water. Our matches were too wet to strike but someone had a lighter and we all smoked cigarettes until the lighter got lost somehow. Then we smoked one at a time in turns, lighting one cigarette from the end of another, so as to keep a light amongst us and make the cigarettes last out. Haveridge was rather interested in classical music and so he and I spent part of the night in cheering each other up and passing the time by whistling or humming such pieces as we could remember. There we sat in the dark, he on a ledge of mud and I on a rusty brazier, both caked with mud, both knee deep in water, both shivering and blue with cold, nothing to be seen but the glow of a cigarette end and the black outline of the trench parapet, nothing to be heard but the occasional whine of a shell or rattle of a machine-gun, and the ceaseless drip of water from our little roof. It is unlikely that Mendelssohn's 'Spring Song' and Rachmaninov's 'Third Prelude' have ever been heard under more strange or unpleasant conditions.

At 3.00 am another man and I were detailed to relieve two men at a water pump some little distance away. The communication trench which led to this pump was then four feet deep in water in places and though we scrambled along it on pieces of board we got in up to our waists. The pump itself was fixed on a wooden platform of duckboards above a sump hole where the water collected. When we arrived the whole platform and the pump were two feet under water and we had to feel for the pump handle. The two of us worked at this turn and turn about without relief for six and a half hours – until 9.30 am – by which time we had lowered the water level to a foot below the platform. The trouble was that more water came in almost as fast as we could pump it out. Also we had to be careful where we stood, for apart from the risk of slipping off the platform into the sump, the place was rather exposed to snipers and as it got light a number of bullets whisked over us or plopped into the mud of the parados by our heads if we stood up straight at one side of the platform. It was tiring work but we did keep warm and when we were relieved at 9.30 am we waded back to our old trench and had some wet bread and a rasher of muddy uncooked bacon for breakfast. The communication trench was partially revetted with sandbags and on our way back a huge section of it suddenly collapsed into the bottom making a great wave of muddy water that almost swept us off our feet. It came up to my chest and almost submerged the other man who was not as tall as I was. At about noon we were relieved by the Glasgow Scottish. We went out past the pump and I saw that the pumping had been discontinued and the platform was again about a foot under water.

We came out of the trenches into Harley Street at Cuinchy and marched right back to billets on the far (west) side of Béthune. It was a most painful and exhausting march and we did not arrive at our particular farm until 6.00 pm when we flung ourselves on the straw, too sore to move and too tired to bother about food. My feet were very tender when we came out of the trenches because they had been in water so long. As my socks dried with the marching and the mud inside my boots formed into little hard dried-up pellets, my feet began to swell with the heat and friction and the soles soon became covered with a mass of the most painful blisters. I smeared my feet all over with Vaseline that night, wrapped them up in old handkerchiefs and they were much better in the morning.

We spent the next four days at Béthune and were mostly occupied with cleaning. Our greatcoats were so thick with mud that many of us plunged them in a small stream nearby and, after tying them to stakes in the bank, allowed them to drift in the water all day. We then wrung them out as well as possible, partially dried them in the sun and scraped the remaining mud from them with our jack-knives. We all carried the old early kind of gas bag respirators which were merely cloth bags to pull over the head and were soaked in sticky chemicals. They had two glass eyepieces and a rubber mouthpiece and valve. The skirt of the bag was tucked in under the collar of the tunic and air was breathed in through the treated material and expelled through the valve. One day we had them tested by the simple method of entering a specially prepared gas-filled hut while wearing them and remaining there for several minutes. If we were affected by the gas the helmets were faulty and we received new ones. On one of these four days we had our first bath in France. It was a poor affair but better than nothing. I describe further on the usual kind of baths and bathrooms that were provided for the troops in France. We got one about every six weeks or two months as opportunity offered.

On 14 December we moved up to reserve billets in Harley Street. On the way up Private Green of our platoon fell out through illness and was taken to hospital. Our billets were in a row of very much damaged cottages on the west side of Harley Street and most of them contained some dilapidated wire-netting beds. These beds were very simply constructed by stretching a length of wire-netting across two horizontal wooden joists about two feet apart. We put our mackintosh sheets on them first to stop the draught and then rolled ourselves up in our two blankets on the top. From 4.00 pm until 9.00 pm on the afternoon of the 14th we were on fatigue, clearing mud from the trenches in the 'Orchard' district which was a little east of Harley Street. We went up to them by way of 'Woburn Abbey' which was the much-shelled remnant of the village church of Cuinchy. Nearly opposite our billets in Harley Street was a large barn used as an Army soup kitchen. Many thousands of tired-out troops must have called in there on their way out from the line to be warmed and cheered by a basin of steaming hot soup. We went in two or three times after night fatigues.

On 15 December we had our first fatal casualty in the Battalion. I was standing by the roadside outside our billet when a small party went past to fetch the tea dixies from the cookhouse further along towards Woburn Abbey. As they were returning a few minutes later a shrapnel shell burst right over them and one man was killed. Part of the shell whizzed past my leg and hit a large stone behind me. I picked it up and found it still hot; it was about one inch thick and two inches long. We remained in Harley Street until 18 December, going on working parties every day. One day we went up 'Wimpole Street' which was a wide trench running off the Béthune to La Bassée road in the opposite direction from Harley Street and leading to Hulluch and Loos. We went back to Annequin on the 18th, had a 'bath' there on the 19th and relieved the 2nd Oxford and Buckinghamshire Light Infantry in the front line on the afternoon of the 20th. This time we went up Harley Street, over Pont Fixe across the La Bassée Canal and up a long deep trench called 'Cheyne Walk'.

We had a very exciting and uncomfortable night. The engineers had moved large gas cylinders into the front line with tubes leading forward over the parapet and just after dark, as the wind was blowing towards the enemy lines, they let off large clouds of gas. We all 'stood to' on the fire step with our gas helmets on and waited. As the gas drifted over to the enemy and they became aware of it the trouble began. 'SOS' signals of red and green lights went up all along the enemy line and they opened a heavy fire of rifles, machine-guns and artillery. We all crouched over our parapet and blazed away at them, being assisted in our aiming by the wood fires they lighted all along their parapet with the idea of making the gas clouds rise and pass over them. Bullets hissed and 'plopped' round us, 'whiz bangs' screamed over us and huge shells rumbled and whined far overhead and crashed like thunder far in our rear. We could not see clearly through the goggles of our gas helmets which were continually getting misty and we could not touch anything without smearing it with the inevitable mud. Exploding shells in front and behind rained showers of loose earth and stones over us and then it began to rain. It almost always happened in France that as the miseries of bad weather increased the danger from the enemy grew less, and it was so in this case.

In about an hour, when it became apparent to the enemy that we were not going to attack, his barrage slackened off and finally ceased. We took off our gas helmets, having worn them for two and a half hours in all, and stood about in the mud and a steady downpour of rain for the remainder of the night. There were no dugouts or shelters of any kind for the troops, but in the very early morning before it was light I found a small place in the trench side containing about 10,000 rounds of SAA (small arms ammunition – rifle cartridges). I managed to squeeze in on top of the boxes and have about an hour's rest.

At daybreak the enemy shell barrage came down again, but this time fell on the support and reserve lines behind the firing line. As we stood with our backs to the parapet we could see the enemy shells that had passed over us, just as a golf ball can be seen when looking down its line of flight. The 'whiz bangs' looked like cricket balls to us because the part we saw was the flat circular base of the shell. In about an hour the shelling stopped, we had our ration of rum and began to think about breakfast. Unfortunately for us whoever had brought up our bread ration during the night in the usual sandbag had fallen into a sump hole with it and turned it into an unpleasant mixture of spongy bread, mud and wisps of rough canvas. However we were cold and ravenously hungry so it all went down along with wet and slippery bits of cold bacon. In the early afternoon we were relieved from the front line and went back to the reserve lines. Our section was ordered to 'Spoilbank Fort', which was a kind of 'strongpoint' as they were called later on, wired in on all sides and capable of independent defence.

An extraordinary thing about this gas attack and the heavy shelling that followed it was that not one man in D Company in the front line was either wounded or killed. To the uninitiated in trench warfare this would surely go to prove that the shelling was not nearly so severe as I have described, but the fact was that the enemy's range was a trifle too long so that the weight of the barrage fell between the front and support lines and by great good fortune not one of the 'shorts' actually landed in the trench. If a shell had actually fallen in one of our fire bays, half a dozen men would probably have been killed or wounded in a second, but the old saying that 'a miss is as good as a mile' was demonstrated many thousands of times during the war and a shell falling on the outside of the parapet or parados – unless it was a big shell – very rarely did any damage to the occupants of the trench.

This sector of the front was famous – or infamous – for expert enemy snipers and for one known as 'Ginger Fritz' in particular. We were warned of him by the outgoing Battalion on our arrival. He was believed to have a concrete or plated sniping post somewhere in No Man's Land to which he crept out before daybreak and from which he sniped at our front line all day. The slightest movement above the parapet in daylight provoked a bullet from him and it was practically useless to attempt to use our small mirror periscopes as he smashed them with a bullet almost as soon as we put them up. The morning after the gas attack we had four of them splintered to atoms and then gave up trying to use them. We were told that a few days before we went in an officer and two sergeants of the Battalion then in the line went out across No Man's Land one morning before dawn with the idea of catching him as he came out. They never returned, but the next day three small wooden crosses were seen planted in the open as a warning to others of their fate.

In the evening after our arrival at Spoilbank Fort we were ordered out to carry rations up to the front line. We each carried two sandbags of dry rations or two petrol tins full of water. They were tied together and slung over the shoulder, and were a pretty heavy load to take for a long distance up the slippery and muddy Cheyne Walk. When we had nearly reached the front line we found that another gas attack was just about to begin and we were ordered to drop our rations and get back to reserve as quickly as possible before the inevitable enemy barrage came down. We raced back as hard as we could go, slipping and splashing along in the dark through the mud and water, but shells were falling on all sides long before we got back to the Fort. After a while things quietened down and Billy Haigh and I and two engineers found a small dugout and had a much needed rest, though we had to turn out periodically during the night and do an hour's guard at one of the Fort entrances.

The next day we moved back to Annequin. It rained heavily that day and at night when another gas attack was taking place and a counter-attack by the enemy was considered possible, we slept in skeleton equipment with our rifles by our sides ready to be rushed up to the front in case of emergency. Nothing extraordinary happened however, except that unfortunately the wind changed and blew some of the gas back over our own trenches. We spent the next day quietly at Annequin and on the following morning, 24 December, a small party of us went up to Cambrin Fort at the corner of Harley Street. Cambrin Fort was a large brick house that had been enormously strengthened by sandbagging inside. Walls of earth-filled sandbags about four or even five feet thick had been carefully built up round the walls of all the rooms inside both upstairs and down, leaving only a small floor space on the stairs and landing and a small square in the centre of each room, except that in each room two or three V-shaped emplacements were left through which to fire. It was cold but dry and safe and we spent the next day – Christmas Day – very comfortably there.

On Christmas morning one of the others and I went down to the canteen in Annequin to buy some tins of fruit etc. and collect our mail. I received a splendid parcel from home containing amongst many other things half a cooked chicken in one of Lazenby's sealed tins. On our way back to the Fort we met General Kellett, our Brigadier, who wished us a Merry Christmas. We reciprocated with great gusto! That night we warmed up the chicken on our brazier and had a good feed of chicken, mince pies, cake, tinned fruit etc. and felt that things were not quite so bad after all. I was pretty well at this time, though all my fingernails had come off, presumably as a result of cold and exposure and through having my hands so often covered with mud. I had mentioned the muddy water in my letters home and on Christmas Day I received a pair of Wellington boots from Father. Under less severe conditions they would have been very welcome and very useful, but as things were it was quite impossible for me to keep them. In the first place they did not reach quite to the knee so they were much too short to be of real service in the waterlogged trenches we inhabited from time to time, and apart from that I was so weighed down already with essential kit that it was beyond me to carry these rubber boots as well.

On the afternoon of Boxing Day we moved back from Cambrin Fort to Le Preôl and after we arrived there I spent all my tea time in hunting round for the Battalion postman. I found him at last and gave him the Wellington boots to return to England. When I got back to our billet – an attic in a small house this time – I was too late for tea but found three more Christmas parcels waiting for me. Shortly after-wards at 6.00 pm the whole Battalion was suddenly ordered out to go back up the line on another fatigue – this time to carry out the huge iron gas cylinders which had been used in the recent gas attacks. We reached Harley Street once more at about 8.00 pm and went up the communication trench, still deep in water, where we had worked our first time on 30 November. It soon began to pour with rain but we worked on until midnight, struggling down the trench with cylinders about four or five feet long that seemed to weigh a ton each. We got back to Le Preôl at 2.00 am soaked through and plastered with mud.

At 5.00 am we were up again, had breakfast and marched off at 6.00 am. I carried the three parcels on top of my kit. I also carried pounds of mud that I had had no time to scrape off my clothes after the previous night's fatigue. Everyone was fagged out and sleepy when we started, but we trailed on with the usual ten-minute halt every hour until 1.00 pm when we almost literally crawled into Belle Rive. I lay on my back in a barn for half an hour after arriving, too tired to move a limb. Later in the afternoon a few of us walked round to a little watchmaker's shop just near and had some coffee. Green rejoined the Battalion that afternoon from hospital, but his face was swollen all over and he looked queer, so I advised him to go to see the doctor again at once, which he did. I never saw him again after that, but I got a letter from him from a convalescent home in England some months later.

The next morning we left Belle Rive at 7.30 am and marched to Norrent-Fontes which we reached at 2.15 pm. This was another most exhausting march which I shall never forget, but I managed to keep going, though many fell out by the roadside and were brought on later in lorries. We reached Norrent-Fontes on 28 December and were billeted in a cowshed for the first night, but the next day our No.3 Section was moved to a little estaminet nearby where we slept on the tiled floor. It was dry and clean and we remained there for the whole of the Divisional rest which lasted until the end of January 1916.

1916

January

We spent the whole of January on rest at Norrent-Fontes, a small village near Lillers, which we had reached on 28 December. We had the usual parades for drill etc. every day, pretty much as in England. One day we went to Lillers for 'baths'. They were the usual sort of thing we always had in France – a cold, stone-floored kind of barn with narrow lengths of half-inch gas piping running overhead. There were groups of six or eight small holes at intervals in this piping and as the warm (or cold) water was pumped through the pipes (generally by hand pump) it squirted through these holes on to the crowd of shivering naked bathers standing below. The men went into the 'bath room' in parties of perhaps eight or twelve according to the size of the place and after the 'bath' scurried back to the changing room to get dry and dressed. At one place the 'changing room' consisted of a wooden platform on the roof of part of the barn with brown canvas stretched round corner posts to form the walls. From there a flight of wet and dirty steps ran down to the 'bath room' on the ground floor. As several inches of snow lay on the ground at the time we went to these particular baths, it was a pretty cold business getting undressed and down to the bathroom. Sometimes the bathroom floor was of grooved concrete and at other places covered with trench boards.

February

Nothing much happened whilst we were at Norrent-Fontes and on 1 February we marched to Aire-sur-la-Lys and entrained for Béthune, where we were billeted in the big tobacco factory on the Beuvry road. The whole of our D Company was in a huge room on the first floor. We slept in rows on the boards and all washed in the yard at a long wooden washboard by the pump. We were there for eight days without a great deal to do, though we went for several marches round the district to Beuvry, Essars etc. There was a large School for Girls in Béthune and, as all the girls had long since left, the baths there were used by the troops. We went one day and found them very different from the baths we were accustomed to. They were all separate little rooms lined with white glazed tiles. One day several of us went to a French cinema in the town. We thought it rather a poor show. The features were all of the domestic drama variety.

On 8 or 9 February we left Béthune in the afternoon en route for the trenches in the Festubert area. Just as it was getting dusk we reached the chateau at Gorre and had tea in the grounds in front of the house. Later we marched on in the dark and after passing through a ruined village which we took to be Festubert, we reached a small stone house near some crossroads where after much delay we were all issued with 'gumboots' that reached nearly to the thigh. We put these on by the roadside, tied our ordinary boots round our necks and moved off for the front line. It would then be about 10.00 pm and very dark. The Festubert area is very low lying and at that time of the year it was mostly under water. There were no ordinary trenches, but breastworks of sods and earth were used instead, so we walked on 'duck-boards' most of the way up with water running underneath them. The way led through an orchard where it was particularly dark and we had to be very careful not to walk off the duckboards into the water below. Just beyond this was a large monument to the Indian troops that had been killed in the capture of 'Indian Village' nearby. Nearer the front line we got off the duckboards and onto an open swampy field with a big dyke running across it. It was rather difficult to jump across in the dark and Haveridge fell in and got very wet.

We reached the front line very late. It consisted of a high breastwork in front with a shallow firing step and a low breastwork behind about three feet high. Beyond this to the rear was the open field and, as it was all under observation by the enemy whose position was on higher ground, it was impossible to either reach or leave the front line in daylight. Hot rations were laboriously carried up in dixies during the night, arriving generally after midnight, and water for drinking was extremely scarce. I well remember Sergeant Morris serving out our water ration one day – two teaspoonfuls per man! The rats there were exceptionally large and numerous and were a continual pest. The first night they ate a hole in my haversack and devoured my rations. They were very bold too: one nearly the size of a cat ran right up to my face as I was looking over the breastwork on guard during the night. When we left the Festubert area thirty-four men of D Company had to be provided with new haversacks as the rats had eaten large holes in their old ones. On the second night Haveridge was overcome by the cold and exposure and had to be partly carried down the line. Later the same night Robertson went out with a small patrol party and never returned. We heard that they encountered an enemy patrol while floundering about in the mud and water in No Man's Land and lost touch with Robertson. It was reported afterwards that he was wounded, captured by the enemy and died in their trenches.

In front of the front line proper were a series of 'islands' about fifty yards apart and perhaps seventy yards from the front line. These were like shooting butts on English moors in size and shape and were each held by three men. They were quite isolated amongst the waste of mud and water and could only be reached at night. I and two others spent a day and a night in one of them. They were wretched places to be in, especially in daytime as there was no room to move about and no shelter against the weather. They were not high enough in front to allow one to stand up straight without being seen and promptly shot at by the numerous enemy snipers. I put my cap on the parapet to dry it during the morning and promptly got a bullet through it. We had no steel helmets at that time. One of the men in the 'island' next to ours tried to creep out at daybreak to get some water, but was shot in the shoulder before he got away and had to be dragged back again by the other two men. It was impossible to get him away in daylight so he had to lie there in the mud until dark when a party came over from the front line and took him off on a stretcher. The three of us in our 'island' got awfully cramped long before nightfall as we had either to stand in a crouching position or else sit in the mud with our legs across each others'. We were relieved after dark and went back to the rest of the Company in the front line proper.

After four days we went back to reserve breastworks near Festubert in front of the orchard. I was on patrol there at night along a waterlogged, unoccupied sector connecting up with the Oxfordshire and Buckinghamshire Light Infantry on our right. Two of us went together along deserted breastworks and over dykes once every hour to a small bridge where we met the Oxfordshire and Buckinghamshire Light Infantry patrol and gave 'all's well'. The graves here were above ground level on account of the water all round; they were in fact mounds of earth covering the dead. A few yards from our sandbag shelter in the reserve line by the entrance to the forward communication trench was a 'mound grave', the earth from the foot of which had become washed away leaving the feet and lower part of the legs of the dead soldier sticking out. Nothing was left on the ankles but the bleached bones, but the heavy army boots still remained hanging on the feet giving a rather peculiar appearance, especially at night. Near here was a deserted shelter and one night, being off guard for a while and our own shelter being crowded, I lay down in it and went off to sleep. I woke up in a little while feeling hot and heavy about the head and on moving to sit up and still barely awake was surprised when a large rat sprang off my forehead and scuttled away outside. Rats were everywhere – big and little – mostly nearly black in colour. One evening I spent half an hour with a spade slashing at them as they ran about on the parapet of the reserve lines.

In an exposed position a little way behind the front line was an old metal yard-pump with a long handle that creaked horribly in use. Getting water from this was a rather tricky business as the enemy could hear it creak and could hit it with rifle fire. About 16 February we went into reserved billets at a farmhouse near La Couture. While there a number of the men who had drunk bad water from shell holes by the front line were ill. About 20 February we moved back on rest through La Couture, Hinges and Gonnehem to Busnes. Soon after we got there snow fell heavily. We had early morning PT in the snow and the usual cleaning up, inspections etc. I got an afternoon off one day and went into Lillers and had a bath. After a few days at Busnes we began to hear a terrific bombardment in the far distance to the south and could see the horizon lit up with flashes at night. This was the beginning of the great German attack on the French at Chemin des Dames.

March

On about 1 March, after about seven days at Busnes, Billy Haigh and I and others were in an estaminet one evening when an orderly hurried in – all men back to billets, pack up and stand by in full marching order, ready for off at once. We paraded along the roadside about 10.00 pm in the snow ready to move. Very cold, we were kept there until about 11.00 pm and then dismissed to billets to stand by with all equipment ready. We slept part of the night in skeleton equipment with packs strapped up. I slept with Haveridge partly covered with newspapers to help keep us warm as all blankets had been collected and taken to the transport. At about 6.00 am we paraded again, marched to Lillers and entrained there.

We detrained at Noeux-les-Mines at dusk and marched up to Petit Sains-en-Gohelle on the Béthune–Arras road. Rain fell most of the way. Petit Sains was very little damaged then; French women and children were still there and some French men still worked in a coal mine nearby. We were billeted in the attic of a small house in a row where a French miner and his big strapping wife lived. Our Section filled the attic. The next afternoon we (Haigh, Haveridge, Roberts and others) had some fancy cakes and coffee at a small patisserie on the main roadside where some French soldiers were also drinking coffee. In the early evening we paraded for the trenches.

D Company was to go into the front line and as I was now a bomber I was to go into a forward 'sap' trench. The French had held the line hereabouts for a long time and we were relieving them and taking over the whole sector of the front so that they could reinforce the Chemin des Dames area. We marched in platoons at intervals to Bully Grenay (Bully-les-Mines) and there entered the 'boyau' or communication trench which was anything up to three feet deep in water in places. This communication trench was a great length – over 2 miles – and ran over a ridge, across a wide depression where the water was deepest, and so up a further slope to the front line which was just short of the top of another low ridge. It was very narrow and tortuous so as to escape being infiltrated, and was revetted in the French fashion and duck-boarded most of the way. We were weighed down with full marching order and after a long and exhausting march our section relieved the French in the forward sap about 2.00 am. The thick mud here was about 12–18 inches deep and the sap was not revetted. Fingerless gloves fastened together by a long piece of tape were issued at that time. I lost one of mine on the way up that night. It got caught on revetment and the tape broke. In addition to my kit and rifle I carried up a box of Mills bombs most of the way (kit 30 lb and rifle 9 lb and bombs 20 lb: total 59 lb). Mills bombs had just been invented and took the place of the French type, some of which had been left there.

This part of the line was very quiet at the time – the French had done very little shelling and told us they had had only one casualty since Christmas – and the French went out of the line over the top and not by way of the waterlogged trenches. The remainder of the first night in the sap was quiet. We did not know which way we were facing or where our own front line ran, but occasional enemy Very lights (star shells) gave us some idea of the position of the enemy. We had a very trying time in these trenches for the first three weeks of March. The weather was truly awful. It was cold and dull during the day and raining or very often snowing during the night. For five or six days of the time while D Company was holding the front line it snowed heavily every night, driving against us as we stood shivering on the firing step and freezing in our greatcoats. The firing step itself was mostly just out of the water, but in the bottom of the trench was nearly a foot of icy muddy water through which we had to wade periodically in our journeys to and fro, so that our feet were constantly soaking wet and our boots oozing with thin mud.

Owing to the shortage of troops on this fresh sector of front that we had taken over from the French, we had no one to relieve us for a time at least and our Company spent twenty-one days continuously in the trenches, never getting farther back than the main support line. This was a great strain on the strength of the men and it was really hardly surprising when one day Cupid (Hicks), though a big, strong, healthy fellow, fainted on the firing step. Haveridge and I kept going by taking occasional doses of Extract of Coca (a form of cocaine) that Father had sent out to me in the form of gelatine capsules made by Savory & Moore Limited. About 100 yards in front of the front line in this sector was a huge chalk mound known as 'Bully Craters' which was connected to the main line by two long saps which ran forward up to and round it. The Craters were often shelled and damaged by 'minenwerfer' (very large trench mortars), and a great deal of digging had to be done to keep the saps passable and the parapet up along the front edge of the Craters. A little later on I became a regular 'bomber' and spent a lot of my time in the Craters, but for the first few weeks I was with the rest of the Company in the front line proper. The usual routine of work during the night was as follows: on guard on firing step, one hour; on fatigue digging in Bully Craters, one hour; sitting on firing step close by sentry to be ready for emergencies, one hour; and then on guard again as before. In this way we got one hour's 'rest' sitting on the muddy step with our feet in water out of every three all through the night.

At daybreak everyone 'stood to' on the step for one hour and at 'stand down' we had our much-needed rum issue. An officer and sergeant came round the line with a tin cup and a large stone jar of rum. We all had to drink our ration on the spot so that no one had a chance of getting a double ration by buying from another. After the rum issue came the issue of rations for the day and then breakfast. This was generally bread and a rasher of raw bacon which we had to cook for ourselves in our mess tin lids over a 'Tommy's Cooker' and a mess tin full of tea. After that some of us got some sleep in any dugout or cubbyhole nearby, while others were told off for fatigues, fetching water in petrol tins, or coke and coal in sandbags, or cleaning up the trenches as far as possible. In the afternoon at dusk we had 'stand to' for an hour again, and then the night's guards and digging fatigues as before. We had a reinforcement of twenty men out from England at this time, but less than a fortnight of this life sent every one of them to hospital. While in the support line we spent part of the day in trench cleaning and most of the night on 'carrying parties', meeting the transport mules about midnight and carrying water, rations and coke up to the front line.

After twenty-one days we were relieved by the 2nd Highland Light Infantry and trailed wearily down the communication trenches to Bully Grenay village, and then on over the hill to Petit Sains which we reached at about 6.00 am. We were all pretty well run down with the cumulative effects of exposure, lack of sleep and being cooped up in filthy trenches for so long, and it was all we could do to drag ourselves and our heavy equipment back to Petit Sains. Unfortunately Billy Haigh sprained his ankle in a shell hole in one of the streets of Bully Grenay village so one or two of us had to help him to carry his rifle and equipment for the last 2 miles over the hill. We had the same billet as before and slept like logs. We heard afterwards that we were ordered out for a fatigue up the line at 10 o'clock the next morning, but that Captain Green (our Company Commander) told the Colonel he had not a man who could do it as we were all dead beat and he refused to turn out the Company. We spent most of the next day or two in cleaning up and getting the caked mud off everything.

April

We remained in this area for the whole of April, never getting further back than Bruay-la-Buissière, and there only once. The usual routine was four days in the front line, four days in the support line, four days in reserve and then back again to the front line. The days in reserve were spent either in Bully Grenay cellars or in Petit Sains billets, and from there we had digging or carrying fatigues practically every night, starting out at about 8.00 pm and returning at about 2.00 am. Our artillery had by this time relieved most if not all of the French batteries in the area and, although the front was still really quiet on the whole, yet there was more activity than there had been when we took over.

Some time near the beginning of April we went back on a short rest through Hersin-Coupigny to Bruay where we were billeted in miners' houses near the top of the steep hill on the west side of the town. The house that I and several others were in was already crowded with refugee miners from Lille in addition to the ordinary tenants, and we were in the attic. While there we had baths at the splendidly equipped bath houses of a neighbouring colliery. This was a colliery district and miners and 'slag heaps' were all over the country between Bruay and Lens, which last town is directly opposite Bully Grenay. Close behind the support line at Bully Grenay there was a large and much-damaged block of buildings at the head of a mine. One morning early several of us got out of the trench and ran across the dip of 'dead' ground to the colliery, and collected sandbags full of coal from some of the wagons that still stood on the railway line close to the pit.

It was about this time that we first saw the new 'Toffee apple' type of trench mortar in use. These were like a very large football in shape with a two-foot tubular stem. They were said to weigh 60 lb each and certainly did enormous damage and made a terrific noise when they exploded. We were all cleared out of the front line one day while the trench mortar experts sent over about fifty of these things as a reprisal for some previous rifle grenade 'strafe' by the enemy. It shut them up for a while. One day an officer from another battalion came up our sap at Bully Craters, left us his cap, belt and revolver, and crawled out in broad daylight with a couple of Mills bombs to bomb the enemy sap opposite. He threw his bombs after crawling close to the enemy line and then came racing back, jumping over our barbed wire and into the sap. We never knew why he did it, though we heard he had been ordered to obtain identifications within a certain period. He seemed to us to be the worse for drink at the time. He told us he had killed the enemy sentry, and then he put on his things and went off down the lines.

Bully Grenay village was shelled occasionally and one day, while we were billeted in cellars under a row of houses there, a shell landed straight in the doorway of an estaminet across the road and one of our men was killed. The cellars of many of the French houses offered really excellent protection as they were made quite differently from the ordinary English cellars. They were like crypts or vaults and had arched roofs, very carefully and strongly built of brick, and were well below ground level with a good thickness of earth above them. When the house above was hit by shellfire and collapsed, it merely made the cellars safer than before by providing a still greater thickness of protective material.

Early one morning when we were in the front line our No. 13 Platoon Lieutenant was found dead in one of the Bully Grenay saps. Apparently he had been sniped just after daybreak while looking over the top through binoculars. He was laid on the fire step in the support firing line – about twenty yards behind the front line – and remained there until the following morning by which time a grave had been dug for him at Petit Sains. During the night a man was constantly on guard near him to keep away the rats. By this time I was a regular D Company bomber and when the Company held the front line we were up the Bully Crater saps. The farthest point in the sap where it rounded the edge of the Craters was more than 100 yards in front of our front line and about sixty yards from the enemy's. Six men (or sometimes eight men) held the Craters during the night and took turns at the lookout posts. At this time the average casualties in this unhealthy spot were one man per night. This was in the later part of April and the reason was the ever-increasing activity of our artillery and trench mortars, which was paid back by the enemy with rifle grenades and 'minenwerfer' principally directed – as far as our bit of front was concerned – on the Crater saps. One night just after dark and without the slightest warning the enemy put down a heavy barrage of enormous 'minnies' on our Crater saps. The front sap was wrecked and the front post blown to pieces in a very few minutes. The two sentries minus smashed rifles and torn equipment came staggering back through the smoke to the second post where the rest of us were at the time. They were too dazed and shattered to tell us anything, so we gave them a drink of tea we had made just before the trouble started and sent one man back to the front line proper with them as they could scarcely stand alone.

Haveridge, who was a lance corporal at this time and in command of the bombers, went back to get orders and report conditions, leaving me in command. Shortly afterwards the enemy range lengthened and the 'minnies' began to crash round our second post where four of us were crowded together, partly under the frail shelter of a little wooden bridge that spanned the sap at this point. Every 'minnie', as it came hurtling down, seemed to be right over the top of us and any one would have wiped out our little party without leaving a limb whole, but some fell just short and some a little over. We were deafened with the roar and showered with earth, but nothing more. Haveridge came up once through the smoke, shouted that we were to stand fast and then disappeared again down the sap. After one very near one, the other three men lost their nerve and started a rush down the sap, but I was at the nearest end and held them up with my bayonet, and they returned to the post.

At last one 'minnie' came down with an appalling crash on the corner of the parapet on my left where the main sap ran forward to the front post. As it did not fall right in the trench we missed the main force of the explosion, but still the concussion was terrific and I was picked up bodily and flung right across the other three men. My face was pitted and scratched all over with particles of grit and powder. My nose began to bleed and actually continued to do so for more than an hour. Before I well knew where I was however, the others were up and away down the sap as fast as they could go. After picking myself up and regaining my rifle, I decided it was useless to remain alone, and followed them back to the front line, though not without looking backwards and upwards every few yards to see if any more 'minnies' were coming over dangerously near. I did not see the other three men again that time in the line as two of them were sent straight down to reserve with 'shell shock' (in other words, shattered nerves) and the third man (Jamie Bailey), after fainting and being brought round with doses of neat whisky, followed them.

Soon after I had reached the front line Captain Green (OC D Company) came rushing up from Company HQ without hat or tunic to find out for himself how things were going. I had lit a cigarette just before he came and he got a light from my cigarette while waiting for instructions from Battalion HQ. In the meantime the enemy had lengthened their range again and now the 'minnies' were dropping just short of or just over the front line itself. Luckily none dropped in, though most of the men and two young second lieutenants cleared out of the immediate neighbourhood very rapidly when they began to drop close. It is pretty useless trying to dodge 'minnies' however, as it is extraordinarily difficult to judge exactly where they will drop and you are just as likely to run into one as to run clear.

At this time it appeared as if the enemy had advanced and occupied the Craters, though it was very difficult to tell definitely as the 'minnies' had rather altered the appearance of it in places and the moving shadows thrown by the star shells were very deceptive. Instructions came up from Battalion HQ that it was to be reoccupied (recaptured, if necessary) as soon as possible and so a bombing party was formed at once. I was the only one of the original party fit to carry on so eight other bombers were brought up from support and, with Petersen as first bayonet man at the front and myself third man, we started slowly and stealthily up the sap again towards the whitish shadowy mound at the top.

As it turned out the enemy had not followed up their barrage so the saps were empty and our precautions were superfluous, but we had quite an exciting prowl round in the dark before this was proved to be the case. Every turn and twist in the saps was taken with the possibility and expectation of finding a bayonet or bursting bomb beyond. When all was found to be clear more men were sent up at once to dig out the saps which had been very much damaged; and this went on hurriedly and without ceasing until dawn. We all worked hard and I was pretty tired by daybreak when the fatigue party was withdrawn and Haveridge, Petersen, five reserve bombers and I were left to hold the posts. Nothing happened during that day; at night the Company was relieved by the 2nd HLI and we all went back to the support lines.

About a fortnight later we were in the Crater saps once more and it was just after daybreak when I and another man were at the foremost post when the enemy suddenly began to shell us with 'whiz bangs'. They must have brought up a field gun very close during the night. It appeared to be firing from their support line and the shells hissed over like lightning, and burst on our parapet and on the Crater mound in the most unpleasant manner. We very hurriedly left the slight shelter of the sap and dived into a hollow in the ground nearby, which was all that was left of one of the original craters. This was very little better than the sap however, and as one or both of us was almost certain to be hit by some of the flying shell splinters if we remained there many minutes, we decided to make a dash for it across the open and over the sandbagged 'step' in the sap into the second post. Immediately after a shell had burst my companion made a rush and got safely over and, after waiting for one more shell, I followed him. He was particularly lucky for although he went as fast as he could he was still in the open just short of the 'step' in the shallow sap when a second 'whiz bang' flashed over and burst a few yards to his right and just beyond him.

We spent Easter weekend in the support line. The weather had much improved by then and on many mornings the sunrises were really beautiful. Patches of flowers could be seen on some of the hillsides and larks rose high and sang even over No Man's Land. At about 4.00 am on Easter Sunday morning I went down the trenches with a carrying party to fetch water in petrol tins from Bully Grenay village. We reached the village before 6.00 am and as we had plenty of time we went first to the little 'confiserie' in an old store house hear the trench entrance where Madame and her daughter still lived (though sometimes in the cellar) and sold oranges, chocolate and biscuits to the troops. It was a lovely day and everybody felt cheerful. After a really good wash (the first for many days) in the yard at the back of the house we went in and ate a tremendous breakfast. I had six eggs, chipped potatoes, many slices of bread and butter and several basins of coffee. An hour later we had collected our tins of water and were on our way back up the line. We always enjoyed and remembered little trips like this.

There is a peculiar freedom about walking in an open street or across a field after a week of grubbing in a deep, narrow and muddy trench. One night while we were in reserve at Petit Sains our Battalion sent up a large fatigue party to do some digging on the Lorette Heights (Notre Dame de Lorette). We had to pass through Aix-Noulette village on the way and as usual at that time of night it was crowded with troops going out on various fatigues etc. The roads in the centre of the village were flooded with water about a foot deep. We had just got clear of this and were proceeding up the forward slope of the road out of the village, when the enemy dropped a 'burst' of light shells on the road just at the head of our column. I was not far from the front of the first party and we scattered in all directions, some into the ditch on the right of the road, some (including myself) flattened against the walls of the houses on the left, and some lying full length on the road itself. The 'burst' of shells only lasted for perhaps two minutes (as was usually the case, the whole point of it being to harass and surprise) and we then reformed and moved on. One man was killed but no one else was hit at all, so we were really very lucky. I was often amazed by the lightness of our casualties on occasions like this. The first few shells seemed right on top of us and the flashes of the explosions were blinding. I should not have been in the least surprised if half our party had been casualties.

At about this time while in the front line and close support line we were very much troubled by enemy rifle grenades. A rifle grenade is something like an ordinary 5th of November rocket in shape but with a short iron 'stick' instead of a long wooden one. The iron 'stick' is inserted in the barrel of a rifle and the whole grenade fired from the rifle by a blank cartridge. The grenade is fired high in the air and comes almost straight down head first. Trenches, however deep, are thus not protected at all if the range is accurate. One fine afternoon I was in the support firing line close to the Company Sergeant Major's dugout, speaking to a lance corporal, the CSM's assistant. After a few minutes I passed on up the trench towards our dugout and a few seconds later a rifle grenade dropped over silently from the enemy lines straight into the trench where I had been standing and blew him right into the CSM's dugout. He died in a few minutes. Another day one dropped just over the entrance to our dugout, but on the top and not in the trench. It blew two rifles to pieces and the concussion knocked Taylor (old Spud Taylor from South Africa) right down the twenty dugout steps. We had a lighted brazier at the top of these steps and it went to the bottom with him scattering red-hot cokes en route. They were as nothing, however, to the remarks he made as he scrambled to his feet again.

May

About this time I was next on the list for seven days' leave to England. The allotment came through from HQ at last and I was due to go on 2 May. On the night of 1 May we were in reserve at Petit Sains and had to go up to the support firing line on fatigue, filling sandbags and repairing the trenches. Great excitement! While working up at the front little Wright very kindly took my place out on the top exposed to rifle and machine-gun fire so that I could work in the trench in comparative safety as I was going on leave the next day. At 8.00 pm on the night of the 2nd I reported at a little hut by the main road at Petit Sains for leave. We were taken to the railhead on motor lorries and reached Boulogne at 11.00 am on the 3rd by a train that crawled so slowly that part of the way we got out of the cattle trucks and walked by the side of it. We crossed by the noon boat with a French destroyer as guard and I reached home that night. Father met me at the Midland Station.

On the night of 10 May I left home again, spent the night in London and reported at Victoria Station at 7.00 am on the morning of the 11th. It was a gloomy party there. On reaching Folkestone we found that no transports were crossing on account of submarines so we spent the afternoon in a wired-in portion of the beach and stayed the night in billets. We crossed on the 12th and I rejoined the Battalion at Hersin Coupigny on the morning of the 14th after spending one night at the wretched 'Rest Camp' on the top of the hill outside Boulogne. The Division was just going out on rest so I was lucky. We went to Divion near Bruay and were billeted in a large room used as a dance hall. On the first night when the mail arrived Haveridge had a parcel from home containing fresh English butter. Everyone was sitting about on the floor, kit was lying about, people were reading letters etc. and after a while Haveridge discovered that his precious butter was missing. We rummaged about amongst the kit but could not find it until at last Billy Haigh, who as usual had been sprawling full length resting after the march, rolled over and the soft and flattened-out remains of the butter were found underneath. After this I took Haigh out to a Church Army hut nearby to have some coffee and buns. Two other fellows there were trying to play ping-pong near our little table and in a clumsy attempt to catch a stray ball Billy Haigh succeeded in tipping up our table and upsetting coffee all over the floor. He was a real Irishman, good natured but hopelessly clumsy and quite incapable of looking after himself as he was so absent-minded. On the same day he lost his own jack-knife.

While at Divion we were issued with new 'C' type gas helmets in place of the old 'B' type. They were both the old-fashioned 'bag' variety that was pulled over the head and tucked in round the neck under the collar. The cloth 'bag' was saturated with chemicals, and they had glass eyepieces and a rubber valve mouthpiece for breathing out. This was long before the 'box respirator' was brought out. After a few days at Divion we went up the line again at Bully Grenay, passing through Houdain on foot. We always marched everywhere about this time – no trains or lorries.

June

At the beginning of June we left the Bully area and marched back to Camblaine Châteleine ('Charley Chaplin') where we were to have a fortnight's rest and Brigade sports etc. were to be arranged. The march was very long and exhausting and we were in full marching order. Our Battalion was the only one in the Brigade to do the whole distance without a stop for a meal – owing to the stupidity of our old fool CO – and our platoon (No. 13) was the only one of the Battalion that reached our destination without having a man fall out. Over eighty men in the Battalion collapsed en route and had to be brought on in motor lorries. Of course the CO rode on horseback. He was not popular, was entirely thoughtless of his men (the worst fault an officer can commit) and left us soon after. After two days at Camblaine Châteleine, when entries for the Brigade sports were just being taken, we were suddenly ordered to move out the next morning. We marched south-east and ultimately arrived at Villers-au-Bois behind Vimy Ridge where we were billeted in Army huts, but on the mud and uneven floor, and without the stretched wire-netting beds that were afterwards used in this kind of hut.

We heard that a few days previous to this the enemy had made a sudden and partially successful attack on the 47th (Post Office) Division (?) that then held the narrow depth of trenches on the edge of Vimy Ridge and had driven them back to the reserve line just on the edge of the very steep decline that fell away down to Souchez. The footing we had on the Ridge was thus almost lost – our Division and probably others as well as a great deal of artillery were rushed up to retain and retake as far as possible. We were moved up into the line the next night – marching through Carency – and I was in front of the line proper in a kind of sap which was really the blocked-up remains of the communication trench from the old reserve line (now front line) to the old support line. The trench was blocked in two places, the rear place only being held by day and the more forward position held by two of us in turn by night. This was a rather 'nervy' spot at night: attacks were expected hourly and it was easy to imagine shadowy forms stealing down the ruined trench towards us. A young 'barrack room hero' and general 'gas bag' who had been attached to our party had soon had enough and after one night of fright asked the officer if he could return to his platoon. He went; we had no use for such amongst the bombers.

After we had been a few days in the line and a few in support in this position, the Royal Engineers taped a proposed new front line some little distance in front of the line we held. One dark and rainy night we were led out over the top with picks and shovels in addition to our fighting kit and spaced out at about five yard intervals along the tape with orders to dig ourselves in. We were under occasional machine-gun fire during the night and I found two bullet holes through my greatcoat next morning. I dug my section about two feet deep for the whole length and then concentrated on one end of it and got down to about six feet by dawn. It was a wretched day, pouring with rain and very cold, and we spent it in the various 'holes' we had dug for ourselves, covered up as far as possible by our mackintosh sheets, and standing and sitting by turns in the mud and water. Rations – cold and wet – were passed or thrown up from man to man from the old front line because the trench we were digging was not sufficiently deep or continuous for anyone to go along it by day.

I was not very well at this time and a curious rash broke out all over my chest, so when we were relieved from the new trench the next night I went 'sick'. I saw the doctor and was sent down by motor ambulance to the nearest field hospital. I had about four days there before rejoining the Battalion and while there all my clothes were fumigated and disinfected. I was treated to a kind of bath of nasty smelling bright yellow sulphur mixture every day, painted on me with a large brush. It was a pleasant rest except for the smell of sulphur and I felt much better when I rejoined the Battalion at Villers-au-Bois.

We were then in reserve and providing large carrying parties up to the support line every night. We left Villers-au-Bois in the early evening at about 6.00 pm and marched up beyond Carency to a large RE dump on the low ridge behind Vimy Ridge itself. From there we carried up rolls of barbed wire and iron stakes, boxes of Mills bombs and (two men at a time) 40 lb boxes of Aminol high explosive for putting in a huge mine the Engineers were preparing to explode under the enemy front line. I knew more about that mine later on. We had to make several journeys each night before trailing back the miles to Villers-au-Bois when it was getting light. We then had breakfast and went to sleep until about noon. There were a few French people left in the village and two or three estaminets where they sold cheap champagne at five francs a bottle. A few of us used to have a bottle or two of this every afternoon and Billy Haigh got quite light-headed on half a bottle one day. He had to be helped back to the hut and told severely to stop laughing, which last seemed quite beyond him.

After about eight days of this we went back up the line but to a section on the Ridge a little north of where we had been before. The route up to Carency was really charming, the hillsides being covered with huge patches of bright-red poppies – millions of them. Carency itself was a wreck without a complete house standing, but still nothing like so flattened out and utterly demolished as the Somme villages such as Pozières, Pys and Courcelette became later on the same year. The section of front line we were to take over consisted of a series of connected and numbered advanced posts. I had previously declined to take a lance corporal's stripe as I had no ambition to become an NCO, but Captain Green informed me I must take command of one of the posts whether I was an NCO or not. I had a small garrison of six men including one lance corporal and two men waiting to go home for commissions! Our post guarded the shaft of one of the mines from which deep underground saps ran forward under No Man's Land and the enemy trenches. Men from a Miners' Battalion were down this shaft tunnelling under the Ridge and were bringing up large numbers of sandbags full of earth and rock that they had dug out and were throwing them over the parapet.

A little excitement occurred one night when the enemy began firing Very lights directly at the parapet of dry sandbags by our sentry post and succeeded in setting them on fire. I got up on the top and emptied several bags of earth on them to put them out. At this time one of our officers was mortally wounded by a sniper while looking over the top through a pair of binoculars. Also about this time, night and morning, we heard the peculiar roll and thunder of hundreds of guns farther south in preparation for the Somme offensive. The sky was continuously lighted up by innumerable flashes, the earth shook and the air seemed to quiver with the restless rumbling and muttering that constantly rose and fell, and rose and fell again, like the rising, breaking and subsiding of enormous waves. I thought the awful threatening growl of the rising and subsiding periods more ominous and sinister than the full roar that followed and preceded them.

After this tour in the line we had a few days rest at Villers-au-Bois. We were to go up to the line again on a Sunday night and in the afternoon the Brigade nonconformist padre came to conduct a service. It was held in one of the mud-floored wooden huts and about forty of us attended. As the last hymn came to an end the padre opened his bag and produced a new and very small Communion Service – one small white tablecloth, two silver cups and two silver plates – together with a bottle of wine and a paper bag of crumbs of bread. He said that we stood in the face of death: we were going forward into the line that night and none knew who would return. He asked that any who could should remain to take Communion. Horne and I and about ten others did so. It was a service to be remembered.

After these few days rest at Villers-au-Bois from about 24

to 27 June, we went up again to the Ridge with D Company, this time in the support firing line on the extreme edge of the drop into the valley. By now the immense 'mine' saps that the miners and engineers had been working at for so long were completed. One sap ending in two forked saps had been dug across No Man's Land and under the enemy front line, and the sap heads filled with Aminol and electrically wired ready to be fired. It was said there were 600 lb of Aminol in the two. The important thing for the infantry holding the line was to occupy and hold the rear lip of the crater formed by the explosion as soon as possible after the mine went up. For this purpose seven other Battalion bombers and I were chosen and were supplied with twenty-four hours' rations and water each, together with cloth bags full of bombs and spades for digging ourselves in along the crater lip. We were also given half a day's rest in a deep dugout together before the time for action.

On the night of 30 June (?), at twenty minutes to 8.00 pm, an RE officer pressed the button on the electric circuit in the support line and the mine went up. Vimy Ridge was said to have rocked from end to end – our end certainly did. The front line had been cleared and every man in the line was down a dugout of some sort, but the rush of air caused by the explosion was so great that even at the bottom of the dugout where we were, perhaps 100 yards from the mine, our candle was put out and our rifles knocked down. After allowing a minute or two for the tons of earth and rock to fall from the sky where they had been blown, we rushed up to the front and scrambled up the great heap of new loose earth to the edge of the crater. The scene was extraordinary and I remember it vividly. The eight of us were spread out a few yards apart along the edge of what appeared in the fading daylight to be a huge chasm. We could not clearly see the far side at all or judge the depth. Behind and below us down the lumpy slope a line of our men were hurriedly digging out our front line that had been buried with the falling earth. Above – and only just above, it seemed – our shells were whizzing over in a heavy barrage onto the enemy support lines. The flash and roar of the exploding shells, the variously coloured lights of the enemy SOS signals, the hazy figures of our men feverishly digging below, our own curiously isolated position perched on the top of a 'new hill' on the brink of a dark vague crater, but still apparently in the middle of the whole commotion; all made up a strange wild scene quite unlike anything I saw later.

July

We worked hard at digging ourselves in during the night after it became apparent that no immediate counter-attack was intended and by dawn I was down more than five feet in one part of my little trench. There was still no serious attempt by the enemy to get round to our side of the crater, but as it got light we saw five or six of them right across on the opposite side apparently in a new trench they had dug a few feet deep. Then we could see the great size of the crater; it was about as large as the Sheffield Lyceum Theatre. An RE officer who crawled up to look estimated it to be roughly 80 feet deep and 150 feet across. We were in a rather awkward position as it became light for we could not move a foot from our several little holes in the ground without being fully exposed to the enemy. Several of our party had not dug down more than three or four feet and so could not stand up at all. The enemy were apparently in a similar state for early in the morning they shouted across in English that they wouldn't fire if we didn't! We didn't, but one of our snipers did. One of the enemy was hit and apparently badly wounded or killed just as they were shouting across to us about what good beer they had! Some had apparently been waiters in London before the war. After this we spent the rest of the day crouched in our little holes.

We were relieved at dusk and the Battalion went back to Villers-au-Bois. After a few more days of fatigues we marched back with the hope of getting the fortnight's rest and refit that we had missed at the beginning of June at Camblaine-Châteleine. After two days we reached a pretty little village (name forgotten) many miles behind the line and D Company was billeted in the outbuildings (cattle sheds) of a large, old-fashioned French farm. The house was solidly built almost like a 'chateau' facing a very large cobbled yard, with the outbuildings running down both sides and with a high arched entrance at the bottom end. The whole place was thus entirely closed when the big gates were shut at night. We were told a Brigade inspection was to take place soon and we spent the first two days cleaning up equipment, mending clothes and practising ceremonial drill, but at dusk on the second day messengers came running round to Company HQ with instructions to cancel parades and pack up. We were to leave for the front again early the next morning. So vanished our promised rest.

Early in the morning we were on the road and after a 3-mile march entrained at a small country station in cattle trucks en route for the Somme. We passed through some pretty country in the train during the morning. I sat on the floor of the cattle truck with my feet hanging outside and ate a cold pork chop Mother had sent me in one of my weekly parcels of food and chocolate. In the early afternoon we detrained at a small station a few miles behind Amiens. We had to help for half an hour in unloading the transport and horses from the train. Then we put on our full marching order and started out on about the most trying march I remember. The main reason for this was that I had just got some new boots which were hard and uncomfortable, and my feet were in an extremely swollen and painful state before we reached Corbic at about 10 o'clock at night. We marched right through the main streets of Amiens past the cathedral and out into the country beyond, halting at about

5.00 pm in the fields by the roadside for tea provided by a field kitchen. Amiens seemed a peacetime city then; trains were running, private motor cars were on the streets and crowds of people watched us march through. After tea we marched on and on while it got dark and we went through villages we could hardly see, with no lights anywhere. We were about deadbeat when at last we got to Corbic and were billeted in small houses in a side street still inhabited by French women and old men.

During the march and while having a ten-minute rest by the roadside just outside Amiens, French women came up selling the usual packets of biscuits and chocolate. One old woman asked me if we were going to the Somme and told me in a horror-stricken voice of the enormous casualties. We had two days rest in Corbic. The morning after our arrival I borrowed a chair and a bucket of cold water from the people who lived in the house and sat in the street for more than an hour with my swollen feet in cold water. It did them a great deal of good and the swelling went down. An old Frenchman lived in the house who showed me the uniform he wore in the Franco-Prussian War of 1870 and told me of the great retreat during which he marched 150–200 miles in nine days; I forget now how far he said it was. Corbic was undamaged then and there were plenty of civilians about. It was very different from August 1918 when I was there again.

After two days waiting we moved up to 'Happy Valley' near Bray-sur-Somme. We heard it was so called because it was never shelled. We gave up our packs (valises) there and left them stacked in heaps on the hillside covered with large mackintosh sheets. We bivouacked on the short grass one night only covered with our mackintosh sheets but fortunately it was fine and warm. While there we saw the remnants of a battalion of another regiment march back into the Valley from the front, led by their band. There was one officer and about forty men! Both hillsides of Happy Valley were covered for miles with battalions of bivouacking troops ready to go up the line. There was the greatest activity in all directions. New roads were being made straight across the country without regard to crops of wheat or anything else. A new railway was already running trains nearly as far as our old reserve line.

This was about 12 July, and the next afternoon we moved forward and bivouacked long after dark in an orchard on the forward outskirts of Carnoy. Carnoy lies in a valley and the march to it from Happy Valley took us over what appeared to be a high flat ridge. We waited until after dusk before marching forward over the edge of the ridge and down the slope to Carnoy. From the high ground before commencing the descent we overlooked – or should have overlooked in daylight – a great sweep of country where hundreds and hundreds of our guns of all calibres were crowded 'axle to axle'. The guns were never silent on the Somme. This evening there was heavy shelling and the innumerable flashes and spits of fire in the dark valley below, and the roll and peculiar 'rocking' sound of the explosions rising and falling, gave us some idea of what we were going into. The country seemed alight and alive with guns.

We spent two nights in the orchard at Carnoy. The day after our arrival was hot and in the afternoon we made a little shelter with a sheet of old corrugated iron we had found, and sat on the grass amongst the trees with our rifles and ammunition lying about or hanging from branches. Suddenly the enemy began to send some big shells over round about, really searching for some of our big batteries and not for us. We were ordered to get into some nearby trenches at once, but I stayed a minute to put my puttees on and was the last to leave the bivouac just before a big shell hit it. When we returned about half an hour later and all was quiet again, I found my rifle in about twenty pieces, my ammunition all exploded, our corrugated-iron sheet all twisted up at the far side of the orchard and our little patch of grass turned into a shell hole about eight feet across and three feet deep. Haveridge was particularly annoyed because in the hurried removal to the trenches he had left behind a copy of the *Bystander* he had just received from home. When we returned odd sheets and small pieces of the magazine were scattered all over the place.

BATTLE OF THE SOMME

The next morning we moved forward into old enemy trenches between Carnoy and Montauban – trenches that were full of enemy troops only a fortnight before – and so I had the possibly unique experience of going into the trenches at the Somme without either a rifle or ammunition. I got both from a casualty dump that afternoon! We were ordered out for a fatigue up the line during the afternoon with instructions to meet the Engineers at Bernafay Wood Corner – 'Hell Corner' it was called, as we found out afterwards. I was a bit late falling in as I was choosing a rifle from the dump of casualty kit at the time, so I fell in with 15 Platoon instead of in my normal place in 13 Platoon at the front of the column. We marched in single file across the open keeping away from Montauban village which was often shelled and was a heap of ruins. We turned left at the cross-roads near Bernafay Wood and eventually halted with the head of the column at Hell Corner and the remainder along the roadside by the edge of the wood. On the road just where I halted a dead man was lying and I kept away from him with rather a creepy feeling. I could see no sign of a wound anywhere but his ear had been bleeding. Just at that moment I heard the rising wail and shriek of a shell and then a simply terrific explosion as an enormous 'Johnson' fell at Hell Corner itself. Now without a second's hesitation I took a flying leap over the dead soldier and dived straight into the wood. A minute later not a living man of D Company was to be seen on the road; all were in the wood. Unfortunately this first shell fell close to 13 Platoon, where I should have been, but was not. Two of our men were blown to pieces and just disappeared in fact. Part of a boot of one was found afterwards but nothing else. More shells of heavy calibre fell but no one else was hit and after about half an hour, as the Engineers could not be found, we returned past Montauban to our reserve trenches.

Trônes Wood was finally captured about this time and the front line ran along Delville Wood, past Waterlot Farm and in front of Guillemont railway station. On the way back to our trenches Private Betts of 13 Platoon was wounded in the leg. We took him back on a Lewis gun limber. Odd shells dropped round about but nobody else was hit. Early the next morning we went up to Montauban village on a fatigue. Not a house was standing but very curiously a large part of one wall of the church still remained standing up alone with a large crucifix fixed on it, just as it had been for years, no doubt, without a scratch on it. About noon that day we moved up into close reserve in 'Longueval Alley', a trench that ran from Hell Corner through a bit of Bernafay Wood up the slope, round the fringe of Trônes Wood and then on to the remains of Longueval village and Delville Wood.

Longueval Alley was in an awful state. It was a German trench and had been shelled to pieces. It was extremely wide and shallow and was soaked in gas and blood and the acrid smell of high explosive. It was full of dead men, both visible – lying about as they had been killed in the trench itself – and invisible – killed and buried with loose earth from the caved-in sides of the trench – and now formed part of the floor in which everyone walked. One man had had his head and shoulders blown away and the rest of his body and internal organs lay about the trench while odd hands and legs of others lay just by. Further up five men lay close together, one leaning back with wide open eyes and mouth, a jack-knife in one hand and a tin of beef held tightly in the other. Another still sat astride a low sandbag wall in front of a cubby hole; he was leaning forward on his arms and remained so for days, though the cubby hole was often occupied.

Nearer the top of the trench was a tunnel about twenty feet long in which a dead man lay full length. The tunnel was very low – about three feet high – and everyone going up the line had to crawl on hands and knees over his body. He was there for more than a week to my knowledge. Others were partly buried with loose earth, hands or feet sticking up in the shell-torn ground showed where they were. In that bit of the trench that ran through Trônes Wood a bodiless head lay on the ground, while two partly buried bodies close by showed a possible owner. These were the sights we saw that first afternoon on our journey up the line in the sweltering heat. These things and the mud and misery of winter are the realities of war which the ignorant describe as 'glorious'.

The day on which we went up was very hot and the combined smells were almost overpowering. Some of the bodies under the floor of the trench had swollen and the result was a springy, cushiony feeling when walking along which gave us a rather queer and very unpleasant sensation. On the way up near Hell Corner we picked up boxes of Mills bombs and our first job was to carry them up Longueval Alley to the front line near Waterlot Farm. Everything that day was overpowering – the sights, the smells, the heat and the shelling. As we reached the fringe of Trônes Wood the man next to me was hit in the back by a piece of shell. I ran to pick him up and bandage him but the sight of his wound was sickening and Horne came up and finished the job. I was not as accustomed to the sight of ugly wounds then as I became later, when I became quite unperturbed at the sight of anything of that sort. The wounded man suddenly became violently angry and almost mad with rage, tore away from us and rushed out of sight up the trench yelling that he would kill all the Germans!

By the time I had got back from the fatigue to our bit of trench about a third of the way from Bernafay to Trônes Wood I was almost too tired and overdone to walk along, and for the first and only time in France had emptied my water bottle. There were numerous cubby holes dug into the sides of Longueval Alley and I lay down to rest in one of these. They were not very pleasant places but were some shelter from the constantly flying shrapnel. The dead lying in the trench were all dark brown, almost black, and I thought at first that they were French Colonial troops as some of these wore khaki then, but I soon found out that they were our men who had been lying there for several days in the great heat.

A few minutes after we got back from the fatigue Haveridge was killed. He was standing in the trench talking to Sergeant Anderson when he was hit in the back by a piece of shrapnel and died almost immediately. He was buried that evening in a shell hole just outside the trench, and a small wooden cross was nailed together and put up to mark the spot. He was one of our little party in D Company who always went together and I was pretty fed up that evening. Haveridge had applied for a commission and had been waiting for his papers to come through for several months. Instructions for him to proceed to England at once reached the Battalion the day after he was killed.

The casualties were enormous. The shout of 'stretcher bearers' was heard every few minutes and we had nothing to do but lie down and wait. Casualties from the front line came down the trench in an almost continuous stream, with the stretcher bearers working in shirt and trousers only on account of the heat. As always during attacks they were terribly short-handed and overworked, and did journey after journey up and down the uneven trench with heavy loads in the sweltering heat and under continuous heavy shellfire. One wounded man crawled past us down the trench on his hands and knees – anything to get out of it, that was the feeling. Badly wounded men on stretchers laughed and smoked cigarettes, and shouted to us as they went past that they would be in 'Blighty' in a day or two. The wounded were the only optimists that day.

We were in this trench for six days as a reserve ready to go up into the front line in case of any emergency, but doing various fatigues in the meantime. We all carried two loose bandoliers of ammunition in addition to our usual 120 rounds carried in the pouches of our equipment. There was no enthusiasm for ration and water fatigues as all such parties had to go down to Hell Corner and pick up the supplies from the roadside a few yards up. The ration limbers came down the road so far but stopped well short of Hell Corner, and naturally were always in a great hurry to get away again. One day we found the loaves of bread etc. tipped in a heap on the bank side; perhaps we were a bit late and the limbers had gone! After the first day the shelling of Longueval Alley became less severe and not so continuous, although in the early morning and late afternoon of every day we caught it pretty hot.

One night we were to go up to the front line digging and two REs headed the column in the trench as we formed up. I was near the front of the column with 13 Platoon and next to young 'Peps' who had been extremely nervy and on edge all afternoon. (I had been sitting in the trench by his little cubby hole most of the afternoon talking to him and trying to keep his mind off the shelling.) When we started slowly up the trench with our rifles and shovels Peps' great friend Alec was several men further up the line. For about forty yards before reaching the fringe of Trônes Wood, Longueval Alley ran in a straight line without any form of traverse and then through a low tunnel about ten yards long. On reaching the tunnel the front of the column halted for a minute to allow the rear men to close up and just at that moment a fair-sized shell shrieked over and burst straight in the trench in front of the two REs. There was the usual blinding flash and roar, the two REs were killed and several of our men badly wounded. I got a small piece in my left leg just above the knee which stung a bit, and Peps fairly went off his head. He yelled that Alec had been killed and he must go to him, but I told him Alec was perfectly all right although I did not know where he was at all. Then he began to shiver and roll on the ground and talk nonsense until at last I got him up and hurried him off down the trench towards the First Aid Post in Bernafay Wood. I got permission to see him safely to the Aid Post as the fatigue was cancelled and the casualties were being evacuated. It was a bit of a job in the wrecked trench in the dark but I kept hold of him with one hand, though he ran down the trench for a few yards at a time, still yelling, and then flung himself on his face whenever another shell came over. I got him there at last and he was led away mumbling by an RAMC corporal. He was a nice boy, only about nineteen or twenty, and after four days complete rest at an Aid Post away from the line he returned to the Battalion quite well again.

They were very busy with serious cases at the Aid Post so I did not bother to report my little scratch. (I worked it out of my leg with my fingers the next morning.) Two or three of us who had brought down the wounded were standing about waiting to see if there was anything else to do before going back up Longueval Alley when suddenly the 'swish' and 'plop' of gas shells began to sound all round and we hurriedly put on our gas helmets. We soon decided to get back up the trench and out of the wood, but as it was about midnight and we could not see at all well with our gas helmets on, four of us joined hands and stumbled about together amongst the tree trunks and shell holes in an endeavour to keep to the flattened-out track that led into the trench proper. After a lot of tripping and shin bashing we got back up our trench and spent the remainder of the night in peace. The next day Captain Green (OC D Company) sent for me to see the doctor as the sergeant had told him I had been slightly wounded. I had not reported it but he said the doctor had better see to it. A few days later when we went back to trenches near Montauban I was sent down to Carnoy Dressing Station to be inoculated.

Another night a large digging party of men from all four companies of the Battalion went up the line with three officers, past the back of Waterlot Farm and out onto the open ground in front of Guillemont railway station, to dig a new trench in preparation for a further attack. The RE officer had no orderly so I went with him while he marked the site of the new trench and got the parties of men spaced out. He left at about 3.00 am and when it came time for us to go the three junior officers with the party sent for me to guide them out and back to Longueval Alley. They had lost all sense of direction, did not know where our trenches lay and offered me a compass to help to fix our position. They formed the men up ready for off and I led them back across the slope to Trônes Wood and so safely into Longueval Alley again. We got back as it became light and had no casualties. We went back to trenches between Montauban and Carnoy after this and remained there two or three days during which time I was inoculated. This would be about 26 July.

Our next move was up into the front line on the right of and beyond Waterlot Farm. We went up in the afternoon through Longueval Alley past all the dead still lying there and across the open behind the farm, where trenches when made were at once obliterated by shelling, and into a long narrow trench more or less facing Guillemont railway station. A company of the 2nd Oxfordshire and Buckinghamshire Light Infantry were already there waiting to go over the top in a big attack at dawn next day. We were to hold the trench against possible counter-attacks after they had gone. The night seemed long and we were all crowded together. Before dawn our artillery put down a most terrific barrage on the enemy lines and it seemed impossible that any men could live in it. At dawn the Ox and Bucks LI went over the top and we never saw them again. It was part of a big attack on a large front in co-operation with the French but we heard that it miscarried. C Company of our own Battalion went over at the same time from another trench but all the officers were killed and only four or five men got back. We heard that Captain Green of our D Company tossed up with the Captain in command of C Company as to which should go over the top in this attack: very fortunately for us Captain Green won the toss.

That afternoon we were heavily shelled and had a number of casualties. I stood talking to Lance Corporal Robertson in one fire bay for a while and within five minutes of my leaving him a big shell came right into the bay and he was killed. During the morning more Mills bombs were wanted as the Ox and Bucks LI had taken all there were and the only supply was at the top of Longueval Alley on the far side of the open stretch of shell-churned ground. I fetched one box, running and diving from shell hole to shell hole, and most of the other bombers did the same. As it got dark at night the shelling became heavier with shells of enormous calibre (12" or 15") dropping every few minutes round Waterlot Farm and shaking the whole hillside. A counter-attack was made on our left but was driven off. At about 10.00 pm or 11.00 pm we were relieved by the 2nd HLI. The first platoon to reach us lost eight men killed and buried in getting across the open ground. Eventually the order came down to us to move out and get away as fast as possible, which we did!

We reformed on the high ground beyond Bernafay Wood and marched back to the same trenches as before between Carnoy and Montauban. We had another day there and in the evening a party of us went forward again to bury the dead who had lain so long in Longueval Alley. There was a certain amount of shelling going on around us at the time and it was altogether a rather difficult and unpleasant job, although somewhat improved by an officer going round first with a large tin of lime. We were formed into parties of three and lifted or dragged the bodies out of the trench and into the nearest shell hole, where they were covered with lime and earth. The next day we left the Somme. About 200 of us marched back to Happy Valley out of the original Battalion of about 800 strong. We received large reinforcements of men and officers there and moved back for what we hoped was our long-promised rest.

August

We were again doomed to disappointment with regard to the rest. After four or five days' marching we found ourselves going up the hill to Mailly Maillet village one afternoon, and that night we relieved the Scots Guards opposite Serre. The Division was to remain in the area between Mailly and Hébuterne until 18 November after the Battle of the Ancre. For the first four days D Company was in the reserve line near the top of the hill. The ground sloped down gradually to the The Apostles – Matthew Copse, Mark Copse, Luke Copse and John Copse – four clumps of tall trees that stood in No Man's Land in the valley. Further to the right was Beaumont Hamel in the enemy lines, and well up the opposite slope were Serre village and Pendant Copse. For the second four days D Company was in the front line. This line was the main support line before the Somme attack on 1 July, but the front line proper had then been so wrecked that it was left unoccupied.

In front of our section of line was a bombing post about fifty yards out amongst the barbed wire, and as I was in charge of D Company bombers I took four men out to this post on the first night. It was approached by climbing over the parapet after dark and crawling through a little tunnel which ran under the first belt of our barbed wire, then going along a little open track amongst the wire until a small clear space was reached, which was marked by two sandbags of earth. We lay here from 9.00 pm to about 4.00 am keeping a constant lookout on all sides. In recognition of this rather exacting watch we were exempted from all fatigues during the day. The first night was quiet but the second night was not. Soon after we arrived at the sandbags and settled down in our lookout positions the enemy sent over one of his big 'minnies', and after that he sent one over about every twenty minutes. They all fell round about our post, shook the ground and scattered lumps of earth over us.

We were constantly on the lookout and saw most of them as they sailed up into the sky from the enemy trenches – the little red fuse could be seen burning in the dark – but about midnight we failed to see one rise or hear it turning as it came down, and it dropped with an enormous roar only a few yards away and wounded three of my four men. Spud Taylor, who was one of my best men at this time, was standing up at the moment it exploded and although he probably weighed 15 stone he was lifted off his feet and flung down several yards away. The wounded were not very seriously hurt and rapidly made their way back to our front line; in fact they had gone before I well knew what had happened. After a few minutes during which all was quiet, I left my one remaining man at the post and crawled back to the front line. I called over the parapet to the sentry to send a message to Captain Green that we had had three casualties and wanted some more men up, and then I returned to the post. I do not know if the message was delivered but no one came and the two of us remained on guard until dawn the next morning.

On the third day some bad water was brought up from somewhere behind the line and a number of men were ill, myself included. That night I went down into the Company dugout and told Captain Green I did not feel well enough to do a night's guard out at the post, but while I was talking to him a runner brought a message that no parties were to go beyond the front line as our artillery was going to shell the enemy new wire and front-line trenches.

The next day I was better again but spent all afternoon before I could find men to make up my party for the sap. It seemed to have got a bad name; about eight men went sick and so got out of it when instructed to go with me. We went out at last though and had a fairly quiet night with only a few 'minnies' and no casualties. We could distinctly hear and occasionally – when Very lights went up – faintly see enemy wiring parties out repairing and renewing their barbed wire. Previously, on 1 and 2 July 1916, an enormous number of casualties were sustained in the attack against Serre and Pendant Copse on this front (amongst others the Sheffield Battalion, 12th York and Lancs were practically wiped out here) and thousands of bodies lay out in No Man's Land, both in and behind our original front line. This was because some of the attacks were launched from the support line on 1 July. The result was that on those warm August nights the bombing post out amongst the dead – who could be distinctly seen lying about – was a rather unpleasant place. After the November attack – the Battle of the Ancre – when Beaumont Hamel was blown up and captured, and 'Munich' trench and the low ridge along which it ran were taken, large fatigue parties with GS wagons were sent down into the valley to collect all the dead, who were buried in large graves or pits near Mailly Maillet village.

A fresh officer from England was appointed to 13 Platoon when we came out from the Somme. He was a quiet, gentlemanly, studious sort of chap and had been through a course in England, but had never been in France before or seen the trenches. On one of the first nights in this sector he stood on the fire step by me in the reserve line looking down into the valley, and when an enemy Very light went up said he supposed that that was a trench mortar! Such men, who knew not the first thing about real trench warfare, were sent out from England at the end of 1916 after two years of war to command men of many months of actual experience and testing in the trenches, who themselves could not get their commission papers through on account of the red tape and needless delay, although in many cases to my knowledge their applications had been made before they left England. The fact was that men of slight qualifications and no experience could get commissions at that time (1916) if in England, but once they were out in the ranks in France then there was an endless delay before they were recalled. This officer was a polite, inoffensive sort of fellow but would never make a soldier, and soon become known to the Battalion as 'Auntie'.

After these eight days – four in reserve and four in the front line – we were relieved by the HLI and went out of the line for four days at Coigneux. We were in huts amongst the pine trees on the top of a hill outside the village. We returned to the trenches for another eight days – four in support and four in the front line – but a little to the left of our first position. There were no bombing posts there and nothing much happened. We went down 'Roman road' where an old French light railway line was laid (and even water pipes!) and were somewhere near 'Egg' trench, and 'Cat' and 'Dog' trenches, I believe. This was rather to the right of 'Valois' trench where I subsequently had a forward observation post. Roman road was perfectly straight and about ten feet wide – more like a country lane than a trench – and we used to go up to the top of it and then out across the open road to a ruined sugar refinery to collect rations. This open road ran along the top of a hill behind the reserve trenches from Mailly to Colincamps and was only used at night as it was within view of the enemy at Serre across the valley.

One late afternoon at about six o'clock a party of us went up Roman road and across to the sugar refinery to collect rations, but were evidently seen by the enemy. Soon after we reached the refinery they opened fire on it with a long-range high-velocity gun (probably about 4") and we were held up in the shelter of a cellar amongst the ruins for about half an hour. Rather curiously we could hear the gun fired – a dull 'bump' in the distance – then two or three seconds silence before the shell came screaming over to land with a great roar amongst the crumbling walls. We got away with our rations at last by making a rush immediately after one shell had fallen and reaching some shell holes on the far side of the road. We then made a series of further rushes between shells until we got back into Roman road.

While we were in the line at this time our cooks came up in support and made their tea and stew there. They did not like it as they had never been up the line before. One day two or three shells dropped very close to them and though no one was hit, one boy assistant cook was shell-shocked and went screaming round yelling that his head was blown off. He was taken away down the line and we never saw him again. Some of the recent reinforcements were fresh out from England and were rather a poor lot. They were all ages and mostly in poor shape physically. I saw several crawling along the trenches on their hands and knees when any shells came over. No doubt they got more used to the conditions after a while.

September

At the beginning of September we came out to Coigneux for four days' rest. We were in the huts at the top of the hill where we had been before. At teatime on the day after arrival I was sitting on the mud floor of the hut eating a tin of peaches I had bought from the canteen when Sergeant Morris of 13 Platoon came in and asked if anyone wanted to volunteer for intelligence work at Division. Several fellows said they would and asked what kind of work it was, but he said he did not know. Just as he was leaving the hut I said I would volunteer as anything was better than bombing. He went out and I heard no more and forgot about it, but two days later on 6 September I was told I had been chosen to go and was to pack up and report to Division HQ at Conin that afternoon.

Before leaving I went across to C Company officers' quarters to say goodbye to my old friend Horne. We had been together since the first days of 1915 at the Hotel Cecil and at 23 Petherton Road, Canonbury, where we and Robertson lodged before we were moved down to our new camp at Romford. Horne was over forty at this time and had been given the opportunity of going permanently down the line to a Base Camp, but he told me he had no one to live for except his mother who was over seventy and he would rather stay up the line as an officer's servant than be on continual road sweeping and loading fatigues at a Base Camp. So he took his chance and stayed. I never saw him again. He was killed about a month later in the support line near Egg trench by a big dud shell that came straight through the roof of the dugout he was in at the time. Robertson was killed at Festubert in February and I was therefore the only survivor of the little party at Petherton Road. Horne was a good man, and a very good and constant friend, and I was very much fed up to hear of this death. So we went on and I continued to be lucky.

I reported to Divisional Headquarters at Conin and found that there were to be twelve men in the new Intelligence Section that was being formed – one man from each of the twelve battalions in the Division at that time. We were billeted for the night in a farm building in Conin and drew our rations from the Divisional Quartermaster. The next morning Second Lieutenant Furlong from Divisional HQ came round to the billet and told us that he was to be in charge of us, that we were to do observation work with telescopes etc. up the line, and that we were to go forward to Hébuterne village in the reserve line the next day. We were a very mixed party, from Ganard, an engineer in private life (of 23rd Royal Fusiliers) to 'Jock', a docker (of 2nd HLI).

Corporal Dixon (1st King's Royal Rifles) was our most senior NCO. We marched up to Hébuterne where we had two dugouts by a roadside on the outskirts of the village. We had an easy time there for perhaps ten days. We had nothing much to do during the day but went up the trenches at night, taking materials and building two observations posts. Hébuterne had been burnt out some time previously and the walls of many of the houses still stood, but the floors, roofs and windows were gone. It was rarely shelled but machine-guns at long range played up and down the main streets at night, and particularly on the crossroads at the entrance to the village.

After we had been there a few days a battery of four 9.2" howitzers were brought up by tractors and took up positions near our dugouts. One was in a small wood about fifty yards away. After firing about ten rounds all the leaves fell off the trees in that wood. Also, the enemy got an idea of their position and began dropping big shells round about; one man was killed and one wounded on the first day. They were not men of our little party, but we were not sorry when the Divisional Headquarters moved a few days later and we moved too. On the first night we went back from Hébuterne to Sailly-au-Bois. We had a lively ride in a half limber at full gallop through some shelling along a shockingly rough road. Afterwards we went on via Acheux-en-Amiènois to Hédauville where we were billeted in an old chateau. The garden at the back had been converted into a wood-yard and the whole place simply swarmed with rats. There was only the floor to sleep on and they would not let us alone. They ran over us, bit at our clothes, knocked things over, ate our rations and scurried and squealed all over the place. At last two of us got out our entrenching tool handles and chased them for about half an hour or more. After that we wrapped ourselves up completely in our clothes and got off to sleep at about 1.00 am.

The next morning Second Lieutenant Furlong came round

to the billet to give us our first lesson in map reading. We left the chateau that day and moved to a hut on the edge of the village where we remained for about ten days. We went out every day learning observation work and on several days made trips on bicycles up to the line past Mailly Windmill. We used to leave our cycles on the grass by the top of '6th Avenue' trench and spend the day going round the trenches with a trench map so as to learn the geography of the sector in case we should be wanted as guides for Divisional officers later on. One afternoon we were coming up 6th Avenue on our way out when a certain amount of enemy shelling began in reply to one of the frequent heavy 'strafes' made by our artillery at about that time. Quite a number of fairly light shells were dropping round and beyond us. We were hurrying along to get out to our cycles when we suddenly overtook a party of officers of the 63rd (Royal Naval) Division in the trench. A shell had burst amongst them right in the trench. The GOC of the Division was lying there killed and a Staff Major badly wounded. There was nothing we could do, so we were ordered out of the trench and ran along the top for a few yards and dropped in again farther along past the casualties. We got safely to our cycles and were soon away.

October

A few days after this we were ordered up the line from Hédauville and took up our quarters in a dugout near Auchonvillers in the reserve line district, about 100 yards from 6th Avenue. We were to man two observation posts and I was put in charge of the forward one in Valois trench in the support line. It was a well-made OP above a large dugout with a straight shaft and a ladder down into the dugout itself which had a strong roof of iron rails and heavy timber. I went up with one of the others every morning at about 8 o'clock and stayed until dusk. We took up our maps and map board, prismatic compass, 'spotter' and telescopes. We watched the trenches for movement, located machine-gun posts and reported on the state of the enemy barbed wire etc. I sent in a written report every night on our return to our dugout. It was really easy but monotonous work at first, although when the enemy finally discovered our post and began to shell it with 5.9" guns it became less monotonous.

The first few days that we were in this dugout at Auchonvillers our rations were rather irregular in arriving. No one seemed to know we were there and one night at about 10.00 pm, when no rations had come for a day and we were quite without anything to eat, several of us went into Mailly Maillet village to see what we could scrounge. We tried various places and eventually got to the Town Major's quarters where we told our tale and collected several loaves, a piece of meat, and some bacon and cheese. We went back across the fields by the Windmill to our dugout and had our feed about midnight.

A big attack had been intended on this front for some time but had been put off for various reasons. Preparations were going on steadily all October as more and more batteries of guns were brought up with heavy shelling of the enemy barbed wire every day, trenches improved and so on. The REs were very busy near our dugout making a huge shell-proof dugout to be used as Divisional Headquarters during the projected attack. Scores of railway rails were laid criss-cross on the top and covered with earth and camouflaging as a protection against the heaviest shells. Three entrances were dug with about twenty steps each and two gas-proof curtains at each entrance. Right down underground were many rooms with floors, walls and ceilings, all boarded with wood, and when the Divisional Staff came up just prior to the attack they brought furniture, typewriters and everything they would require. The attack – the Battle of the Ancre –

did not take place until 13 November and in the meantime we were kept busy all October observing and reporting day by day.

During this period my reports on the progress of the artillery in cutting the enemy wire were noticed at Divisional HQ to differ very materially from the reports of the artillery observers themselves. They said the wire was well cut, while I reported that it was still extremely thick, especially in front of one section of the enemy front where they had a particularly formidable 'strongpoint' known as The Quadrant. One day General Walker, GOC 2nd Division, came up the line to our observation post in Valois trench himself, accompanied by the GSO 2, to get first-hand information on this most important point. They both inspected the wire through our telescopes and the General asked me how long I thought it would take the infantry to get through the wire in front of The Quadrant. I told him I thought it would take twenty minutes even without opposition and that under machine-gun fire I considered it practically impossible; the GSO 2 agreed. The General then said he thought it would be best not to attack The Quadrant itself but to try to nip it out by advancing on either side. I believe this was ultimately done. If this was so our persistent reports did some good in saving the useless sacrifice of many lives. The wire at this point appeared to be six to eight feet high and many yards wide – a perfect jungle. The artillery were constantly blowing quantities of it up in the air, but there was so much of it that it could not be dispersed and mostly came down again in a more inextricable tangle than before.

As October advanced the front trenches at the bottom of the slope became more and more impassable with mud and water; sections of the front line had to be abandoned altogether. There were many cases of men having to be hauled out by a rope being passed under their armpits. Valois trench itself was three feet deep in slimy water at the southeast end and trench boards were floating about like rafts.

We were provided with thigh-high rubber waders, but the water at this corner of Valois trench was so deep that it came in over the tops of them as we went up to the observation post every morning, and left us with sopping clothes for the rest of the day. It was freezing cold sitting in our little OP looking through a telescope all day under these conditions, so we avoided the corner by getting out of the trench onto the top about fifty yards short of it and running across the open and slithering down the side into Valois trench just near the OP. The enemy snipers had a shot at us once or twice but we were never hit. We used to take up some blackcurrant jam as part of our rations for the day and make hot blackcurrant tea on a 'Tommy cooker'. That and dry bread with a hot rasher of bacon constituted our usual midday meal.

Toward the end of the month we were shelled almost every day with 5.9s and after the machine-gun post, the signallers' post, the special fresh water tanks and everything else but our OP in Valois trench had been blown in and wrecked, it appeared to be only a matter of time before our own little position would be demolished. The point that concerned us was whether or not we would be in it when the end came. Fortunately we were not. We arrived as usual one morning and actually got a yard or two further up the trench before we realized that we had passed what had been the entrance to our OP. A huge shell must have hit it fair and square and it was a most complete and utter wreck. The heavy timber posts at the entrance were split and bent so that we took several minutes to squeeze our way in. The large joists and iron rails of the roof lay split and twisted like hairpins in all directions. The shaft down to the dugout was impassable with pieces of roofing and rubbish of all sorts that had been blown in. Our 'spotter' had been left overnight and was broken in two, jammed between two of the collapsed roof girders. Our lookout slot was blown away and there was nothing to be done, so after a good look around we returned to our dugout near Auchonvillers and reported to Divisional HQ.

No attempt was made to rebuild our OP as it was then the end of October and the attack was to take place in November. I and two of the others were told that we were to be Divisional guides during the attack and the other members of the Section were to be Divisional runners carrying despatches from Division to Brigade. During October I was ill for a few days with a kind of influenza and spent two days lying in the dugout by our little coke bucket fire with my top coat and blankets wrapped round me, trying to keep warm. With its hard dried mud floor and smoky little brazier it was not a very comfortable place in which to be ill. We had no beds of any kind and not very appetizing food. We used to soak the big hard 'dog biscuits' in water overnight and then cook them in bacon fat in the morning for breakfast. Only five of us were up at the dugout all this time doing the observation work while the remainder were back at Divisional HQ. I do not know what they did there except bring up our rations every day.

November

A day or two before the attack we reassembled and moved to the big HQ dugout where we had a little room with two wire beds for the twelve of us. About the same time final preparations of all kinds were being made. Sections of cross trenches were filled in here and there to make more level tracks for the advance of the big tanks that were to take part. A great number of batteries of guns of all calibres were moved into position in the rear, while some gun positions were dug even forward of our dugout so as to be ready for the anticipated advance. One or two 15" guns and one 17" gun were included, and it was said that the Duke of Connaught came up to inspect them. The barrage each day now was terrific – shells seemed to fill the air overhead at times – and of course it was perfectly apparent to the enemy that a big show was pending. While going through some of the main support trenches one day I came across D Company of the 24th Royal Fusiliers (my old Company). I asked if Hicks (Cupid), now Sergeant Hicks, was with them and found him in a little dugout. He was just as bright and cheery as usual. It was the last time I saw him as he was killed in the attack on 13 November.

On the afternoon of the 12th, General Walker and all the Divisional 'G' Staff came up to the dugout. The typewriters began clicking, the signals buzzing and the place was like a big hive. At about midnight the last despatches, plans and dispositions were ready to be taken to advanced 99 Brigade Headquarters (Brigadier General Kellett) which were situated in a dugout in a forward trench on the far side of Roman road, not far from Valois trench. They consisted of two large rolls of maps and papers about two feet in length, and I was ordered to take them. They were extremely urgent – the attack was to commence at about 6.00 am – and of the utmost importance. I carried a Divisional badge and had priority of passage over anyone and everyone in the trenches. The distance through the trenches was about a mile and a half and fortunately it was fine, but 6th Avenue along which I had to go was crowded with men going up for the attack and other troops were going forward along the top by the side of it. I ran the whole of the way where the trenches were open and cleared my way past the streams of men by shouting 'Gangway, Divisional Despatches' every few yards so that they all kept to one side and gave me room to push on. Further up, the cross trenches to Roman road were already damaged in places by enemy shellfire; they were deep in mud and tangled with new telephone wires that had just been run out by artillerymen and signallers, so the going was very heavy. I reached Brigade HQ and delivered my despatches in a quarter of an hour, and in about forty minutes was back again at Divisional HQ. The shelling was only slight at the time although one big 'wuff' dropped right into the middle of the cross trench to 6th Avenue, about two traverses in front of me and blew the whole traverse to pieces, so I had to scramble out and run along the top to get round the charred and reeking mass of earth.

BATTLE OF THE ANCRE

The morning of the 13th broke dull and foggy. The roar of the guns was deafening as zero hour approached and at zero (6.30 am, I believe) the countryside shook as the huge mine at Beaumont Hamel went up. After that nobody at Divisional HQ knew for hours what had happened or how the attack had progressed. The fog did not lift and the aeroplanes were useless so that all the elaborate arrangements for signalling from the ground to aeroplanes went by the board. The conditions for an infantry advance were awful. The trenches were full of water and the mud made anything like rapid movement impossible, while the fog caused endless confusion and loss of direction and touch. Fortunately for us we had nothing directly to do with the attack and really had a quiet day, though I remember we all found it rather trying standing by waiting to be called upon for some job at any moment.

By afternoon we knew that things were not going very well and that little progress had been made. The members of the Staff that we saw from time to time in the dugout all looked worried and tired. Meals taken in for the General all came out again untasted. Everyone crept about as quietly as possible and spoke in whispers. The General could occasionally be heard pacing up and down waiting for news. Everybody's nerves were on edge and there was a general uneasy stir every time anyone came down the dugout steps. I had another journey out to 99 Brigade HQ during the afternoon, but most of the shells were dropping further forward and nothing could be seen of the fighting on account of the fog. It was one of the safest but most uneasy days I ever spent in the trenches.

The front was fairly quiet during the night but the barrage began again early in the morning when another attack was made on Munich trench. I think this trench was mostly captured that day (the 14th). In the afternoon I had to go into Mailly Maillet village to meet the General of another Division at the main entrance to the church and guide him up to our Divisional HQ. I waited there for more than an hour but he did not come. When I got back I found that someone had made a mistake about the time of his arrival and he had gone up earlier by another route. While waiting on the church steps I saw an officer wearing a shoulder badge marked 'Official Cinema' or some similar title (I forget exactly). I had quite a long talk with him and he told me he had been up in front of Auchonvillers with his cinema camera trying to take photographs of the attack, but had been unable to get anything owing to the fog.

At about 11 o'clock that night Second Lieutenant Furlong came for me again and took me in to see Colonel Deeds (Divisional GSO 1). He asked me if I knew the way to a particular trench beyond an open, shallow kind of lime quarry called 'White City' which was at the end of 5th Avenue near the front line. (5th Avenue ran down towards the front line roughly parallel with 6th Avenue, but about 300 yards further south.) I did not, for the simple reason that this part of the trenches was not included in our Divisional front at the time we had been learning our way about. In fact, the Division had side-stepped to the south by one brigade frontage only a few days before the attack. He then asked me if I could read a map and as I could he showed me on his large-scale trench map where this particular trench was. He gave me instructions to meet a Colonel of a battalion of the East Lancs at a house by the church at

Mailly Maillet village at midnight that night, and to guide the Battalion from the village up to this trench by 6.00 am so as to be ready to advance to the attack from there at 6.30 am.

The Battalion belonged to another Division altogether and was being brought up to Mailly Maillet that day. It was rather a tall order as none of them knew the district at all and I had only seen the last part of the route for two minutes on a map. In addition it was a pitch dark night and the shelling was continuous, though not heavy. I reached the village safely and found the Colonel and other officers in the house by the church. The men were resting in the narrow streets nearby but in proper order and all ready to fall in and march off. The Colonel was not coming up with the Battalion but was to be guided up the line by Smith (one of our Section who had come with me) to meet the Brigadier of 99 Brigade for a short conference before rejoining his Battalion in order to take them over the top from the trench to which I was to bring them. After Smith and I arrived he had a long talk with his officers and I had to point out to him twice that we had no time to waste if the Battalion was to arrive in time for the attack.

It was well after 1.00 am when the men fell in and we started off with much clatter through the cobbled streets. The Adjutant was in command and I walked with him. We moved off by platoons at intervals and I got them past the windmill on the outskirts of the village in quick time when I told the Adjutant what a favourite place it was for heavy shells. The entrance to 5th Avenue was amongst a clump of big trees about a quarter of a mile from the road and the windmill, across an open unmarked stretch of ground like a huge field, with no track to give any trace of direction. Here my difficulties began but I judged an angle from the road and struck off to the right across the grass. In a minute we had lost sight of the road behind and could see nothing in the pitch dark but grass on every side. I kept straight on and after about five minutes' steady walk was relieved to see the big trees by the entrance to the trench looming almost on top of us. We had to go slowly for there were 800 men behind us and to lose touch in the darkness would have been fatal.

My instructions from Colonel Deeds were to lead the Battalion along the top by the side of the trench and not in the trench itself, and so we set out to do this. I very soon found that on account of the cross trenches to be jumped by every man in the dark and the innumerable artillery and signal wires that lay across the top and tripped up man after man as they moved forward, now in single file, we would not reach the front line until long after daybreak. It was half past two before we had been a hundred yards along the trench top and so I asked the Adjutant to order the men into the trench. After that we got on much better, although progress was always slow as we had to keep halting to allow the men in the rear to close up. This is always the case where a large party of men have to move up a more or less damaged trench. Part of the way along we ran into a little gas shelling but this was not serious and gas helmets were not put on.

The way lay right down 5th Avenue along which I had once been a short way – but in daylight which is a very different thing from night-time when everything seems changed – and it was not long before we reached a part of the trench that was quite strange to me. This did not matter so long as there was only one trench, but we soon came to a fork. Both trenches appeared to lead pretty well forward so far as we could judge from the commencement of them, but the name board of the left one was missing and the name of the right-hand one was quite strange to me. The right-hand was the wider, more important looking trench, but I understood that 5th Avenue itself led right up to the White City so I chose the left. We got on very slowly after this as the trench was narrow and deep, thick with mud and fairly knocked about in places with shellfire. It wound about a lot and at one corner was blocked to a height of quite four feet by the bodies of several men lying partly buried in the collapse of the trench sides, evidently the result of a big shell. Every man had to climb over this obstruction one at a time and it delayed us a good deal. I had made the right choice at the fork, but it was 6.00 am as we came out of the trench into the open of the White City.

The trench which was to be the jumping-off place for the Battalion started from the opposite side of the White City which was about forty yards wide, but the whole place had been blown to pieces and the difficulty was to see where this trench began. In the grey half light of the early morning many places looked to be the beginnings of trenches, but they were only the blown-in remains of cubby holes and shelters. I was anxious to get the Battalion into their trench because I knew, though they did not, that our artillery barrage prior to the attack was to begin at 6.15 am. After a hurried search we found what proved to be the beginnings of the right trench and I stood at the corner of it until the whole Battalion had passed in. As the last company came up our barrage commenced. At the last moment a message was passed along for 'the guide' and the Adjutant came hurrying back to shake hands and thank me for leading them safely up. Rather decent of him, I thought. I was only a private then.

I had intended to get back quickly but just as I turned to go the enemy barrage descended, so I promptly gave up all hopes of getting across the White City to 5th Avenue and looked around for a temporary shelter near at hand. Everything was blown in except one shelter which was quite large and was evidently used as a reserve dump for Stokes Mortar bombs. It probably contained about 500 of them but I crept inside and lay on them, and hoped for the best. If a big shell had hit it we should have all gone up together. However, I was very tired and soon went off to sleep. When I woke up again half an hour or so later it was quite light and a wounded man (one of the Battalion I had just brought up) was crawling into the shelter. We sat there for a while (he was hit in the hand only) and then as the shelling was dying down we made a dash for it and safely reached the comparative shelter of 5th Avenue. We raced up this at top speed until we reached a small dugout where we stopped for a few minutes to get our breath. We soon pushed on again and at about 8.30 I reported at Divisional HQ.

On the way up the last part of the trench I passed a stretcher party carrying one of our wounded. The stretcher bearers were two German prisoners and our men were walking in front and rear. The Germans were carrying very carefully and steadily; they always did for obvious reasons. The next night I had to lead up another battalion (I have forgotten which) from the village to the same trench, but it was not so dark and as I knew the route it was a simple matter. Nothing much happened and I got back to Divisional HQ in good time. The fog had cleared away by now and we spent part of each day observing the front though our telescopes from a splendidly built, solid concrete little OP made by the Engineers for the use of the General, just across the trench from the big dugout.

On 18 November what was left of the Division was relieved. We came out of the line and moved back on rest. We were ordered to guard the Divisional stores etc. so we were fortunate in riding on big lorries all the way back. On the second day's move we stopped for half an hour in the morning at a village on the route, and then I saw the remnant of my old Battalion. I came across Hugh Trenchard of 13 Platoon D Company (my old Platoon) and heard from him what a terrible time they had had. Poor old Cupid (Sergeant Hicks), Sergeant Morris, Sergeant Little, Private Anderson, Private Bradbury and many others had been killed. Trenchard himself was one of the very few survivors of the old original company that had left England just a year before. We continued to move back right away from the line and about the end of November reached the tiny village of

Cornehotte near to Crécy, on the fringe of the famous woods where the Battle of Crécy was fought by the English under the Black Prince.

December

We were billeted in a large barn at Cornehotte where we had good rations and an easy time. We had PT before breakfast, normally a fairly long walk in the morning and anything we liked for the rest of the day. I went one day to Crécy village and saw the statue of the Blind King of Bohemia which stands in the village square. Another day we tried marching on a compass bearing through a part of Crécy Wood. Once we had a 5-mile cross-country run. The idea was to get us fit and strong for the next show up the line.

On about 10 December, six of us were detailed to go in two motor lorries away up to Hersin-Coupigny, beyond Bruay, to fetch back some Divisional stores that had been left there since May when we were in the Bully Grenay district. It was a day's run to get there in the big 3-ton lorries and we remained there for the night and finished loading up the next day. By teatime that day we got back as far as Bruay and parked the lorries for the night in a big open space on the east side of the town. The others decided to sleep in the lorries on the top of all the stores, but as it was very uncomfortable and cold there, Simonite and I went off to see if we could get a good feed and somewhere better to sleep. We got some coffee and eggs at a place near the station and then wandered along a road on the extreme edge of the town where there was a row of small houses. We knocked at the door of one and asked if they knew where we could get a bed for the night. They said they had a spare mattress and could give us a shakedown in the kitchen if we liked to stay there. It was dark and raining so we promptly went in and they made us very comfortable indeed. There was a man (a miner), his wife and a little boy, and they told us they had another son with the French Army at Verdun. We had some rations with us and they made us coffee for supper. They then lit a fire in the little kitchen, brought down the mattress and also a big eiderdown, laid them on the kitchen floor, and we had a very warm and comfortable night. In the morning they gave us coffee and jam with our bread and when we left refused to accept any payment whatever. We left them what remained of our rations (we always had plenty at this time), gave two or three francs to the little boy and came away after thanking them for their hospitality. When we got back to the lorries we found the other men half-starved after a cold, uncomfortable night, trying to warm some breakfast on 'Tommy cookers'. We soon started off again and got back to Cornehotte that night.

Near our barn was a cottage where a woman lived with her four small children. Her husband was with the French Army. We often used to go in there for coffee in the mornings and often in the evenings too. We sat by the fire, practised our French on the children, had eggs and chipped potatoes for supper, and generally made a sort of little club of the place. I was the only one who could speak any French, but Corporal Dixon had a dictionary and was trying to learn.

Christmas was fast approaching and we decided to make arrangements for a really jolly good Christmas dinner. We arranged with the French woman to hold it in her cottage and we subscribed about fifty francs amongst ourselves to buy extras of all kinds so as to make it as 'Christmassy' as possible. We had or own dixies for cooking for the Section and we also borrowed pots and pans from Madame. We saved up a good large piece of beef from our rations and plenty of vegetables. We bought a duck and a bottle of rum from Abbeville, two lots of preserved cream and a lot of cigarettes from the BEF canteen. We were issued with special Christmas rations consisting of a goose and a large tinned

Christmas pudding. Our own cook, Corporal Catchpole, helped by Madame, got everything ready. We had different things cooking in our own dixies on our earth oven in the field, on Madame's fire in her kitchen and on the fire at the little cottage belonging to our barn. Corporal Catchpole made fancy dishes with buns, jam, whipped cream etc.

Altogether we had a very good time. That was the second Christmas I spent in France and it was much more enjoyable than the first which I spent in Cambrin Fort at the corner of Harley Street near Cuinchy. We saw the old year out at Cornehotte. Corporal Dixon, who was a Roman Catholic, persuaded several of the men to go with him to the next village at about 11.00 pm on the night of the 31st to attend an RC mass and procession of some sort. It was a very cold night with several inches of snow on the ground and for some reason not explained the mass and procession did not take place. They returned very much fed up at about 1.00 am on New Year's morning.

1917

January

We remained at Cornehotte until 9 January. We were out every day walking, playing football etc. and spent the evenings either at the little cottage nearby talking to the four Thiercelin children, Marie Louise, Louis, Rejine and Emile, or else at another house at the end of the village where Corporal Dixon and I used to go to play chess. He was very interested in chess and carried a small pocket set about with him. We went on many evenings at about six o'clock to this quiet house at the bottom of the lane and played until about 8.30 pm, when we generally had eggs and chips for supper before returning to our barn for the night. I remember that little Louis Thiercelin, who was about seven years old, was learning the Catechism and I used to sit by the stove with the book and hear him recite it.

The largest establishment in the village was a farm with an estaminet in the farm buildings. It was the only estaminet in the village and was generally pretty busy during the hours it was allowed to be open. We never went at night but often in the mornings. One morning Simonite and I tried some yellow, syrupy looking drink they had. We did not know what it was called but they served it in small coffee cups half full at 50 centimes a cup. We rather liked it, had four cups each and then set off for our barn for lunch. We soon found that our drink was rather stronger than we had anticipated and halfway up the lane Simonite collapsed in the hedge bottom and could not get up again. We eventually reached the barn and Simonite lay down on the straw without bothering about anything to eat and slept the whole of the afternoon. I had some lunch and then went out for a good long walk. We found out the next day that we had been drinking yellow Chartreuse.

We left Cornehotte on the 9th and marched 17 kilometres to Bernaville. 'Jock' Sullivan was more or less drunk when we started and had a bottle of 'vin rouge' in his haversack so it was not very surprising that he fell out about 5 kilometres short of Bernaville and was left by the roadside. This kind of thing could scarcely happen with men in a battalion, but we were a small independent party, responsible to nobody but our officer, Second Lieutenant Furlong, and he was rarely with us, having many other duties in Divisional HQ. It was getting dark and raining when we reached Bernaville and we were billeted in a barn on a lane at the end of the village just off the very wide main street. The next morning 'Jock' arrived with a long rambling tale of what he had done the night before and with a message for me that a friend of mine would come to Bernaville that afternoon to see me. It turned out that after we had left him by the roadside he made his way – as of course he would – to the nearest estaminet and there in the evening he found a party of the Queen's Own Yorkshire Dragoons, including my old friend Bertie Foothill. When Jock told them all about our Section and every member of it, Bertie thought he recognized me and gave Jock the message. We were staying the day at Bernaville so in the afternoon I went back a short distance down the main road and met Bertie coming along on a bicycle. He was the one and only pre-war friend I ever met in France and I was very pleased to see him. We had a long talk and tea at a patisserie at the corner of the main roads before he went back to his village again at about eight o'clock.

The next day we left Bernaville and arrived at Marieux in the afternoon. It was 28 kilometres but we went on motor lorries so were not tired. It snowed and rained most of the day. From there we moved forward to Aveluy two days later. This was another 28 kilometres which we marched this time, but without our heavy packs which were brought up in the transport. We came through Bouzincourt which was not very extensively damaged at that time, and on through Aveluy village down the hill across Aveluy causeway to 'Crucifix corner', and then up the hill to the right on the road to Ovillers and La Boisselle. A little way up the hill we turned off from the road to some Cromwell huts on the right-hand side. One of these huts was to be our billet for the next seven weeks. A Cromwell hut is a large wooden hut frame with a pitched roof and a covering of tarred felt. It has a door at either end and ours had wire beds along both sides and would accommodate about thirty men. As there were only twelve of us we used one end of it and some other men attached to Divisional HQ occupied the other end, leaving a few spare wire beds in the middle. In the passage way down the centre of the hut and near our end was an old French stove with an iron pipe leading through the felt roof. A Cromwell hut is a very cold place in winter as there is no flooring and the felt is the only covering on the frame for both roof and sides. We therefore kept our stove going as well as we could all day and part of the night for most of the time we were there as the weather was extremely cold.

We were nearly half a mile beyond Aveluy village itself, on the reverse slope from the enemy on the next hillside, and separated from the village by a long, narrow and shallow kind of lake which was crossed by the famous Aveluy Causeway. This was an artificial 'lake', perhaps 2 miles long, and made by the French purposely flooding the valley some time previously. When the water was clear old German trenches could be seen at the bottom of it. It varied in width, averaging about a quarter of a mile, and the only crossing was the causeway which ran straight across from the main street of the village to Crucifix Corner, so called because of the large crucifix still standing amongst a few big trees at the road junction at the foot of the hill on the east side. It was no doubt very advantageous to the French to flood this valley when they did, but afterwards, when Albert was captured and the enemy retired further east, it was a considerable drawback as it compelled all the transport and traffic to cross by the one causeway which was well known to the enemy and almost constantly shelled.

The day after our arrival at the Cromwell huts was a Sunday and in the afternoon several of us crossed to the village, turned left along the railway and made our way into Albert, returning in the evening by the same route. Albert is a fairly large town and as the French had been careful not to shell it when it was occupied by the enemy it was not very seriously damaged. The exception to this was the famous cathedral which had been shelled early in the war by the Germans and from the huge tower of which the great statue of the Madonna and Child hung head downwards. Albert lies in a valley and the tower and hanging statue could be seen for many miles on all sides. Most of the masonry immediately at the foot of the statue had been shot away and the great metal framework that still held it to the tower could be plainly seen bent over into the shape of an enormous hairpin. On reaching Albert we made our way from the station to the square in the centre of the town where the cathedral stood. Enormous blocks of stone lay about as they had fallen and on looking up it appeared as if the statue itself would come crashing down at any moment. Some civilians were already back in Albert and had opened small shops. After buying a few small things we wanted, we hurried away as it was getting dark. During the next three days we had nothing much to do as far as Intelligence work was concerned as there were no observation posts on the new Divisional front. The cold was extreme and remained so throughout January and until 16 February.

On the Tuesday after our arrival it snowed very heavily and made it quite impossible for us to construct any OPs in the usual way. In the first place the ground was frozen like iron and apart from that any digging or building would have at once shown up to the enemy against the snow. We soon found that we were not to have altogether peaceful nights. Each night at about 8.00 pm, and again at 1.00 am and 3.00 am, large shells came screaming over our huts to crash into the houses of Aveluy or, falling short, to plunge into the 'lake' below us or onto the unhealthy causeway. They were mostly H Vic (high-velocity) shells said to be fired from an armoured train that came up to the enemy front each night. They made a very disturbing noise as they passed close over our frail hut. One night one was very short and fell between the next two huts farther up the hillside than ours, pretty well making matchwood of the lower one. It came over at about 1.00 am and woke us all up. Everyone in our hut was unhurt, however, and as there was nothing to be done and nowhere else to go we stayed in bed and hoped there would be no more. The next morning I found that two splinters of shell had come through our hut felting close to my bed and torn four small holes in the blankets I was wrapped up in but had missed me somehow. One piece of shell fell out of my blankets as I got out of bed. I was lucky once more.

It was on 13 January that we reached Aveluy and our Cromwell hut, and on the 16th I started with an awful cold and cough that continued for more than a month. On most days it snowed, every day and night it froze, and we soon began to run short of wood for our stove. A party of us went out every morning looking for wood, particularly amongst the old trenches and dugouts in the neighbourhood. Late at night, after our stove had gone out, everything in the hut seemed to freeze. One night I left some cold tea in a mess tin and the next morning it was a lump of brown ice. My top blanket was frozen stiff every morning with pieces of ice breaking and falling out of it when I got up. The inside of the hut roof was white over with frost and long icicles hung down over my bed from the inner framework. The insides of my boots were white with frost in the mornings and my air pillow froze stiff except just where my head lay. The 'lake' over the old flooded German trenches was frozen over with ice a foot thick and we walked across the ice to the Albert side. During the day I always wore thick gloves and at night I had on all my day clothes except socks, boots and tunic; in addition I had my tunic, top coat and two blankets wrapped round me, and wore a cap comforter and thick bed socks.

On the 18th, Second Lieutenant Furlong took us up the line to the West Miraumont dugouts close to Courcelette which was as far as it was possible to go in daylight. The ground over which we passed on our way up had been won yard by yard at the cost of enormous casualties during the Battle of the Somme the previous summer. It was so torn and scarred by innumerable shell holes that scarcely a square yard of unchurned soil remained. The heavy rains, followed by severe frost and snow, had turned this battlefield into a waste of hard frozen, water-filled shell holes. Some were joined together to form irregularly shaped miniature lakes, some divided by crests of ice-bound earth. All were confused and tangled by the refuse of war – barbed wire, stakes, planks, broken-down limbers, dead horses, shell cases, ration tins, ammunition boxes, steel helmets, smashed stretchers, rifles – all discarded and now frozen hard into the earth and ice. For the first part of our journey up we followed the remote road past the ruins of Ovillers (marked by a name board), across the dip in the ground by 'Fritz's Well' and on through the village of Pozières, which we should never have known was there at all except for the noticeboard by the roadside.

At Pozières we left the road and walked on a duckboard track that wound and twisted amongst the shell holes for about a mile and a half, before bringing us at last to the six entrances to the series of underground galleries known as the West Miraumont dugout. This was the largest 'dugout' I ever saw. It had six parallel shafts running down into the ground at a gradual slope and these were all joined up laterally by four long, level galleries or wide passages, one below another. Some sections of these galleries had wire beds on either side in two tiers; other sections were widened into rooms and used for Signals, Aid Post etc., and later on as advanced Divisional Headquarters. We returned to our hut by the same route in the afternoon, hurrying along the duck-boarded part as this was directly under observation from Lonpart Wood, a high wooded ridge at that time well behind the enemy front line.

The next day we went up to West Miraumont dugout again to get a clear idea of the route in case we should be required as guides later on. It was 4 to 5 miles each way from our hut. There was a little shelling round Pozières and further forward but we had no casualties. For the next fortnight no observation work was possible and we were put on salvage work among the old trenches and gun emplacements near Divisional HQ, which was on the top of the high ground above our huts, roughly halfway between Ovillers and La Boisselle. There was a competition between divisions as to the value of the materials salvaged and our Division recovered more than £1,000 worth.

February

On the night of 2 February we went up to the front line for the first time. The condition and arrangement of the front held by the 2nd Division at this time was most extraordinary and exceptional. It was also most unpleasant and uncomfortable. There was no trench system at all – none. The whole divisional front was held by twenty-one isolated small posts with about six or eight men in each, and there were no support or reserve lines or posts behind them. The men actually in support were accommodated in the huge West Miraumont dugout and in other smaller dugouts in Courcelette village, and in case of attack would apparently have had to deploy in the open. The twenty-one posts of the front line were dotted roughly along what had been 'Regina' trench, which had been captured by the Canadians the previous autumn when Pozières and Coucelette were also taken. They were about fifty yards apart and about half a mile in front of the West Miraumont dugout. As there were no trenches or breastworks it was impossible to reach any post in daylight, but a cinder track could be followed across the snow at night to one of the posts and two tapes (one black and one white) laid along the ground led the way to the others. The white tape was intended to show the route when the ground was dark and free from snow, and the black tape when frost or snow made the white one invisible.

We set off from the Cromwell hut after dark and took the usual route up to the West Miraumont dugout. At about 9.00 pm we left there and went forward past the ruins of Courcelette and up a sloping track that took us on to a prac-tically flat stretch of open country across which the cinder track wound over the snow. It led first to a dump ('B' dump) of wire, stakes, etc. and then on to one of the front-line posts – No. 8, I believe. There we divided into two parties: the one I was with turned left and visited Posts 8 to 1 and then back again to No. 8, while the other party visited Posts 8 to 21 which were closer together than the others. It was a clear fine night and the moon was full so that we could clearly see where we were going. We followed the black tape over the snow as it wound round shell craters and across ruined old trenches. We were completely out in the open 'on the top', within perhaps 100 yards of the enemy posts, so no one spoke or made any unnecessary noise. We were practically on the top of our own posts before we saw them but as they knew we were coming round and, as we had one of their own NCOs as a guide, we had no trouble or difficulty, just a whispered word or two and we passed on. As all movement had to take place after dark and, as the district was so featureless and difficult to recognize in any way, all along the front a single wire fence had been put up just in advance of the posts to keep men from accidentally wandering into the enemy lines.

We heard no rifle or machine-gun fire the whole night and were told that this was a recognized understanding with the enemy on this bit of front, as it also was on various other sectors at different times when the conditions were sufficiently hazardous and miserable without being added to by perpetual sniping. However, this understanding did not extend to the artillery as we very soon found out. There was not a great deal of shelling, but what there was was very much more dangerous than usual because we were quite exposed instead of being sheltered in a trench. The shells that came over made no shell holes as the ground was so hard that they burst immediately on hitting it and merely made a blackened patch in the snow. The cinder track was well known to the enemy and on our way back from the posts at about 1.00 am they suddenly began to shell it. We heard the first one or two coming and flung ourselves full length on the ground as they crashed on and near the track just beyond us, sending splinters hissing in all directions. There was no shelter anywhere and when some more followed the first almost immediately, we gave up our quiet walk back and ran as hard as we could go until we reached the corner by the West Miraumont dugout again. Fortunately nobody was hit and we got back to our hut at 3.00 am, rather tired and with no wish to visit the front line again.

The conditions for the men who held the front posts at this time were very severe. The cold was intense and they had very little room to move about. No hot rations could be got up to them; they went into the posts for forty-eight hours and took all their rations with them. Cases of 'trench feet' were very common and after one spell of extreme cold all the divisional transport had to be sent up to bring down the men who had held the posts as hardly any were able to walk. Of my own old D Company in the 24th RF, 'Alec' (the friend of 'Peps' who had shellshock at the Somme) got 'trench feet' very badly and had to have both feet amputated in hospital. There were many cases like that.

On the night of 5 February enemy aeroplanes dropped bombs over our area and killed six mules in the transport lines near our hut; afterwards they came over almost every night and sometimes during the day. On the night of the 6th they dropped about twenty big bombs and also fired machine-guns at the night transport going along the road nearby. On the night of the 9th they killed eight mules and one horse of the 17th Royal Fusiliers transport that were picketed about eighty yards from our hut. It was not very pleasant lying on our wire beds during all this commotion and wondering where the next bomb was going to land. We could hear their engines humming, the crackle of their machine-guns and the bang of our own 'Archies' (anti-aircraft guns). Every now and then there was a roar and our hut shook as a bomb burst somewhere in the vicinity. Sometimes a mule screamed or a transport man shouted but all kept as quiet as possible; not a light was allowed, all fires were put out and we lay and listened as they passed and repassed over us until the hum of their engines finally died away in the distance. What particularly annoyed us was that we had to put out our fire whenever they came over and were then left to almost freeze for the remainder of the night.

For a long time batteries of howitzers and guns of all kinds and calibres had been taking up positions all along our section of the front; the crossroad by Fritz's Well was lined with howitzers. Our attack was finally fixed for 17 February and was to be a big attack, including many other divisions besides ours, and great preparations had been made. As aeroplanes had been so useless in the previous big attack of November 1916 owing to the fog, it was decided not to rely on them this time for information about the course of events. Our party of observers was to be used instead, to go forward over the top after the first attacking waves, and to get all information possible about the positions reached all along our Divisional front, the degree of success attained, the reinforcements or ammunition required and so on, and to report by a chain of runners to Divisional Headquarters as early as possible.

To do this we should have to pass through the enemy barrage several times and advance into the open exposed to all the rifle, machine-gun and artillery fire there might be. On the day before the attack we were therefore supplied with a new kind of suit of armour called the 'Dayfield Body Shield – Army Pattern', to be worn over our clothes but under our equipment. It was supposed to be revolver bullet proof and shell splinter proof, and was in two parts. The first part was a large, thick-padded collar, strapped round the neck and under the arms, and was mainly to help carry the weight of the second part which consisted of a number of cloth-covered sheets of spring steel shielding different parts of the body. One large sheet of steel covered the front of the body with two smaller separate sheets below to cover the front of the legs. A second large sheet covered the back with one wide separate sheet below to cover the back of the legs. After these had been hung on by straps over the shoulders, a strong waist band was tightly fastened round to cause the spring steel to bend more or less to the shape of the body and so present a curved surface to a bullet or splinter of shell from which it might glance off without penetrating. These body shields were undoubtedly a considerable protection but they had two very great drawbacks. Firstly they were very heavy, hot and tiring to wear, and secondly they upset the wearer's normal balance so that on

1. Trench warfare on the Yser, 1915.

(West Yorkshire Regiment)

2. It seemed as if nothing could possibly exist in that inferno. Photograph of a German trench after the bombardment, first day of the Battle of the Somme, 1 July 1916.

(West Yorkshire Regiment)

3. A German trench battered by British artillery, Ovillers-la-Boiselle, July 1916.

(West Yorkshire Regiment)

4. Longueval village after the battle for Delville Wood, July 1916.

(West Yorkshire Regiment)

5. Moving up to the Flers line, Battle of Flers, September 1916.

(West Yorkshire Regiment)

6. Ammunition being carried to the front line on the Somme, Winter 1916.

(*West Yorkshire Regiment*)

7. 8th Battalion, West Yorkshire Regiment, returning after the capture of the Mont de Bligny in the Battle of Tardenois (28 July 1918), for which the Battalion was awarded the Croix de Guerre.

(West Yorkshire Regiment)

8. Second Lieutenant Stanley Spencer MC. (*Edwin Hadley, Sheffield*)

muddy and uneven ground it was difficult to avoid numerous falls. We all felt top-heavy in them and at the slightest slip on the muddy ground their weight brought us down before we had a chance to recover.

On 16 February, being YZ day (the day before the attack), we started off up the line at 3.30 pm wearing our Dayfield body shields and 'fighting order'. ('Fighting order' was skeleton equipment with haversacks strapped on the back in place of packs.) Marching in the body shields was very exhausting and we did not reach the West Miraumont dugout until 7.00 pm. That evening the great thaw set in after the long frost and it rained heavily. The result was that the hard ground was covered with a thin coating of slippery mud. The night was pitch dark and at 9.00 pm, after an issue of rum, we moved off over the top to a dugout (the only one there was) not far behind the front line. It had been a Company HQ and was now being used as advanced Brigade HQ. This dugout had two entrances which were connected by about twenty yards of good deep trench, the only bit of decent trench I ever saw in the whole area. The rest were the broken-down remains of the 1916 trench system which we had captured from the enemy. We reached this dugout at about 10.30 pm and remained sitting on the steps of one of the entrance shafts for the rest of the night – cold, tired and in the dark. Troops were coming forward throughout the night to take up their attacking positions along the front in readiness for zero hour which was 6.00 am, I believe.

BATTLE OF MIRAUMONT

It was rumoured afterwards that two men of the King's Royal Rifle Corps went over to the enemy during the night and told them of the impending attack. However that may have been, the enemy certainly did know and at about 5.00 am put down a very heavy barrage all along the line, causing enormous casualties amongst our crowded troops who were lying out in the open waiting to attack at zero hour. At 6.00 am our guns of all calibres opened up with a terrific barrage and the attack commenced. The morning was dull, misty and very wet. It was impossible to see more than two or three hundred yards.

Our Section was divided into two parties: the first under Second Lieutenant Furlong included Lance Corporal Goff and three men as runners; and the second under Second Lieutenant Miller of the HLI included myself as acting NCO and three more men as runners. Each officer carried a list of code words (girls' names were used) representing messages as to reinforcements, casualties, ammunition required and so on. If the officer became a casualty the NCO was to take the code list and push on, sending back information by the runners. Fortunately we had no casualties during our forward tours and everything worked pretty smoothly.

Our party started out first at about 7.00 am and hurried straight forward across our own front line through the enemy barrage and into the enemy positions just captured. We soon saw the terrible effects of the early enemy shelling. Scores and scores of our men lay killed and wounded where they had been waiting through the night for zero hour. At one point we came across the advanced aid post where eight RAMC stretcher bearers lay dead, all piled up together. We left our three runners at about this point and Second Lieutenant Miller and I went forward beyond the second enemy line on the left flank of our Divisional front picking up what information we could. We then returned to the runners and sent off our report before making our way back through the barrage again to the Brigade HQ dugout which we reached at about 10.00 am. The shelling was heavy all the time and we had many narrow escapes, but we were lucky as usual. In one of the German trenches I found a loaf of hard 'black bread'. It was very hard indeed and very dark brown but not really black. It had been left rather conspicuously on the parapet and I did not taste it.

We came across one casualty who had been killed by a shell which took off the top of his skull completely, but without damaging his brain apparently. I stopped a few moments to examine his brain which was grey and in little wavy wrinkles or creases, just like photographs of the brain I had seen before. However, shells were crashing round about and Second Lieutenant Miller was anxious to get on, so I had to hurry after him, sliding and stumbling under the weight of my cumbersome body shield. The RAMC stretcher bearers worked heroically all day as they always did, making journey after journey under heavy fire right back to the West Miraumont dugout where the first Field Dressing Station was. There was no cover for them and they had to go slowly and steadily over the top all the way with their heavy burdens of wounded: they had many casualties.

The second party under Second Lieutenant Furlong got safely back to the Brigade dugout at about 11.30 am and the whole party of us remained there until about 6.00 pm when we were ordered to return to the West Miraumont dugout for the night.

Unfortunately, before this happened, we had two casualties in our little section. Corporal Dixon and Jock Sullivan had not been forward with either party, and while we were away Jock had been scouting around and found a full jar of rum somewhere. Army rum is extremely strong stuff and it was not long before they both became more or less drunk and consequently careless of becoming exposed outside the protection of the bit of trench. Shells were continually raining round the dugout which was apparently well known to the enemy as a headquarters of some sort. When Jock climbed on the top just outside, very tipsy and shouting that he would fight the whole German Army, he very soon got hit and came rolling head over heels into the bottom of the trench again. His Dayfield body shield was badly dented and probably saved his life, but he was also hit in two places in his arm which was broken. Corporal Dixon also got a large piece of shell in his left arm. They were both immediately dragged down the dugout steps where the rest of us were bunched together. They were difficult to manage on the steps and we could not get anywhere near the bottom as it was full of wounded. I bandaged them both up with field dressings and tied up their arms with puttees; later in the afternoon the RAMC got them away. I never saw either of them again but we heard later that they both got safely to England. They were really lucky to be wounded for otherwise they would probably have been court-martialled for being drunk whilst in the line.

We had an exciting journey back to the West Miraumont dugout at 6 o'clock. It was dark when we started and the shelling was still very severe. Just as I got out of the trench on to the top I heard a big shell hurtling up and I promptly flung myself down full length beside the body of a man who had been killed there during the afternoon. The shell burst just short and a piece of it hit him and made him lurch over against me but I got off without a scratch. I got up again at once and hurried off after the others but we soon lost touch with each other and I made my own way back, diving to the ground several times as huge shells burst unpleasantly near. Once I crossed a large shell hole which was frozen over, but the ice was weak with the thaw and I went through, getting soaked to the waist in icy water and having some difficulty in scrambling out again.

The next morning we went back to our Cromwell hut because our part in the attack was over. The enemy had been driven back a considerable distance and was now entrenched along the foot of Lonpart Ridge. The attack was stopped because of the mud and bad weather, and preparations were at once begun for a further advance as soon as possible.

On 24 February I went up to Divisional HQ for a week in charge of Maile and Jackson who were to act as orderlies for staff officers going up the line. They were both required during the first night however, so at 4.50 am I went up the line with Captain Gervais who was on the 'G' Staff. We went as far as Pozières in a Daimler staff car and nothing much happened. I got back at 10.30 am but had to start out again at 12.30 pm, this time with Second Lieutenant Furlong. He had just been awarded an MC for his work in the Miraumont attack the week before, while Lance Corporal Goff and a private in our Section both got the MM. Second Lieutenant Miller and I were recommended for the MC and MM respectively but we got nothing.

On this second journey we went up first to the West Miraumont dugout and then forward, but to the left on the high ground overlooking Pys and directly opposite Lonpart Wood. It had been raining heavily most of the previous week and the ground was like a morass. The dead on the recently captured ground had not yet been collected and buried, and lay about all over. When we reached the highest ground we were seen by enemy snipers and had to dive very hurriedly into the nearest shell hole where we were hung up for some time. We eventually got away by a series of short dashes from shell hole to shell hole, one man at a time, and bullets hissed past every time we made a move.

March

On 5 March, when Divisional HQ moved forward to the West Miraumont dugout, we left our Cromwell hut and moved with them, being accommodated in one of the numerous subterranean galleries. On 7 March we started proper observation work once more. Simonite and I went forward very early in the morning to 'Grundy' trench on the forward slope facing Lonpart Wood. During the previous night a large fatigue party had brought up a great many boxes of SAA (small-arms ammunition), rifle grenades, Mills bombs and Stokes mortars, and had dumped them on the hillside just outside the trench. As soon as it was light the enemy saw the new dump and began to shell it. After a few minutes it caught fire at one end and rifle ammunition began going off in all directions. The main part of the dump was almost on top of the dugout used as a Company HQ and if the dump had gone up the dugout would almost certainly have caved in under the explosion. There was a considerable stir amongst the few men near as we all rushed out on to the top and formed a chain passing smoking boxes of Mills bombs etc. from hand to hand until they were dropped into a part of the trench which was deep in water. In this way we cut off the main part of the dump from the burning boxes and the danger was averted. Soon afterwards it got very hazy and misty and the enemy ceased to shell. We were lucky again.

The ground was in a terrible state at this time on account of the thaw. Parties had often to go out with planks and ropes to pull men out of the mud where they had sunk waist deep or even farther. I saw two men limping to the Aid Post with cut and bleeding feet wrapped up in handkerchiefs. They had got stuck in the mud up the line while wearing long gumboots and could only escape by leaving the boots in the mud. On 8 March Simonite and I were given a free choice to go where we liked to report on certain enemy trenches near Lonpart Wood. We set off before daybreak and climbed to the top of a ridge on the right of the Divisional front near Le Sars village. Here we found an old disused trench called 'Gallwitz' trench with an excellent view of our objective. The enemy must have seen flashes from the lens of our telescopes for we were shelled after we had been there about an hour. In the meantime we had got all the information we required so we slipped down some steps into an old dugout until the shelling stopped and then made our way comfortably back to HQ just as it began to snow.

A further general attack was fixed for the 10th at 5.15 am, so at 6.00 pm on the 9th several of us went up the line to 'Greyvillers' trench to be ready to watch and report. We had our telescopes and a field telephone with a wire straight through to 'G' Office at Divisional HQ. Although the morning was dull and hazy we were able to observe movement after about 6.00 am and report without loss of time. This attack was only partially successful and not much advance was made. We returned to HQ at 3.00 pm and the next day Simonite and I went up to Gallwitz trench again. On 12 March Simonite and I went beyond Greyvillers trench and further forward to a recently captured enemy trench called 'West Weg'. Early the next morning I was there again (with Jackson this time) and I saw through the telescope some of our own troops advancing up the slope and right over the top of Lonpart Ridge. The enemy had gone. I immediately went back to the nearest signals dugout and telephoned the news to 'G' Office, Divisional HQ.

The enemy was now steadily moving back day by day and the famous 'retreat from Bapaume' had really begun. On the afternoon of the 13th I accompanied Second Lieutenant Furlong and Colonel Deeds (GSOI of the Division) round the lower part of Lonpart Ridge, and the next morning Simonite and I, Lance Corporal Goss and Maile went up the Ridge again. The enemy were now putting down a terrific and continuous barrage all along the top of the Ridge and into Lonpart Wood and we were unable to get over, but early the next morning we went up once more and reached the level ground on the top in full view of Achiet le Petit and Achiet le Grand. On the 16th it was too misty to see anything so we went back as far as Grundy trench and spent the night in a small German dugout there. The following morning Simonite and I went forward past Lonpart to the Biefvillers line and saw columns of smoke from all the villages the enemy had set on fire. Simonite was bilious and ill that day, and Lance Corporal Goss evidently had no wish to take any risks by going forward further for information. I therefore left them both in a dugout by Lonpart Wood and went forward alone past the Biefvillers line and over the railway past Biefvillers village to the Company HQ of the Middlesex Regiment who were the most advanced troops we had. I got all the information I could from the Company Commander and saw that Bapaume in the valley away to the right was on fire, as also were the villages of Achiet le Petit, Achiet le Grand, Bihucourt, Biefvillers and Avesnes. I then returned to the others at Lonpart Wood.

I went into the wood later and saw some of the enemy sunken big-gun emplacements from which they used to shell us at West Miraumont and Aveluy, and read one of the range cards giving the ranges in metres to various places behind our lines. In the early evening the Queen's Own Yorkshire Dragoons came up and went off at a gallop round Achiet le Petit which was then a great column of smoke. Later on the Bengal Lancers came through and went straight forward over the Biefvillers line. They looked very weird and fearsome with their long lances with red and white pennants, and with their black faces and flashing teeth. Some wore steel helmets and some white and red turbans; they led horses carrying Hotchkiss guns in parts. We went back to West Miraumont dugout after this and had a couple of days' rest. I had strained my right knee in the mud a few days earlier and it was causing me a certain amount of trouble so I was glad to take it easy.

The enemy had retired so far that we were completely out of range, so several of us took the opportunity of looking round the ruins of Courcelette. Not a single house or even part of one was left standing and the church was a heap of stone and rubble. Some broken pieces of gilded candlesticks and remnants of blue silk vestments were lying amongst the heaps of masonry. Nearby amongst other ruins were a great many torn and rain-soaked books, all in French of course and apparently upon religious subjects. We guessed that the curé's house had stood here. Along the lower ground at the bottom of the slope from the church a light railway used to run. The battered engine still remained on the track where it was when the village was captured by the Canadians. (A very well-known drawing reproduced in the illustrated papers during the war showed the capture of Courcelette by the Canadians with this engine in the foreground.) The next day we walked across to the small village of Pys. It was also a complete ruin. In the centre of the village was a large mound perhaps twenty feet high and partly grown over with weeds: this had been the church. At one time it must have been a rather pretty village, but in March 1917 it was a silent, gloomy collection of ruins, overgrown with dank weeds and heavy with the smell of decomposing bodies.

The 2nd Division was relieved about this time and on 22 March, after hanging about all day, we left the West Miraumont dugout for the last time at 6.00 pm and marched back en route for Hédauville. My knee had been painful all day and by the time we reached Albert at about 8.00 pm I was scarcely able to stand. Fortunately I got a lift on a RFC tender from there to Hédauville and eventually reached our billet, 'Barn 47', at about midnight. My knee was still very painful the next morning so I 'went sick' and on 24 March was admitted into the 2nd/1st South Midland Casualty Clearing Sation at Puchevillers as a case of 'synovitis'. This CCS consisted of about twelve long huts; the patients slept on stretchers placed on low trestles and had four blankets each. I had nothing to do except go to the Dispensary Hut once a day and have my knee painted with iodine, so I had a very restful, lazy time. The doctor came round each morning with the Head Matron and examined all the patients. After a week my knee felt much better and I was anxious to get back to Divisional HQ as my commissioning papers were coming through, but I had to ask the doctor on two morning inspections before he would allow me to leave the hospital.

April

At last I got away on the evening of 5 April, though with my knee still in bandages. The train of cattle trucks left Puchevillers at 7.00 pm and rumbled into Abbeville at 1.00 am. We had to get out there and as the next train did not leave until 11.00 am we wandered off to try to find somewhere to spend the remainder of the night. There were about half a dozen of us, all from different regiments, and no one knew where to go, but after a while we came across a man who directed us to the YMCA hut. We went there and found it open though in darkness, so we went in and slept on the floor in our top coats. The next morning I caught a train on to Étaples and spent the night at the huge Rest Camp on the sands. We were in bell tents there and I went into one of the big refreshment rooms for a good feed at night. The favourite game here seemed to be 'House' played by large parties on the sands. Each player buys a card for 1d* printed with numbered squares. These cards are all numbered differently. The banker then draws perhaps twenty numbered tickets from a bag and the player who has most of the drawn numbers on his card wins.

The next morning all the men for the 2nd Divisional area were marched down to the station at 7.00 am. The train eventually crawled up at 11.00 am: this was the usual and expected kind of thing with these troop trains. When it did get going again it took two hours to reach Saint-Pol-sur-Ternoise, a distance of 30 miles. Here we detrained once more and spent another night in a Rest Camp, this time in long wooden huts. In the evening I got a pass out from the camp and went into the town for a meal. The following morning (8 April) we moved on again. This time we got as far as Bruay and from there I walked the last few miles to Beugin where the Observation Section was billeted. In this

---

* One 'old' penny (0.42p)

extraordinarily tedious and roundabout way I reached my Section after three days and nights. The distance as the crow files from Puchevillers to Beugin is about 30 to 35 miles!

The following day was 9 April and Easter Monday, but as the Division was now going back into the line, we moved forward as far as La Comté and on again to Haute Avesnes the next day. The weather was bad – it snowed on the 10th and 11th – but my knee kept up pretty well. It was on Easter Monday that the Battle of Arras began and the Canadians captured the whole of Vimy Ridge. As we moved forward day by day the roar of the guns became more and more distinct, the road surfaces worse, the traffic more congested and all the usual signs of 'something doing' more evident. On the 12th we reached Maroeuil and on the 15th I was put in charge of the Divisional Transport to lead them up to Roclincourt. We went down the main Arras road as far as Sainte-Catherine and then turned north again on the Lens road to Roclincourt A week earlier Roclincourt was almost in the front line but when we arrived it was about 4 miles behind.

VIMY RIDGE

We slept in a large dugout the first night and early the next morning Robertson (of the HLI and now in our Section in place of Jock Sullivan) and I went forward right over the top of Vimy Ridge to find a suitable position on the forward slope for use as an observation post. It was just getting properly light as we passed over the crown of the Ridge and saw for the first time the immense expanse of undulating country beyond. We had a little excitement at once as a string of mules, which was being led forward near us carrying ammunition to the 18-pounder guns, was spotted by the enemy who at once opened fire from one of their batteries. Shells came thick and fast and we raced for shelter to one of the old enemy gun emplacements while the mules went tearing off back over the Ridge completely out of control and were soon lost to sight. My instructions were to find a suitable position with the best possible view for a Divisional Observation Post and having selected one, to make a sketch on the spot of the view obtainable, and to return to Divisional HQ the same day.

After the shelling had stopped we wandered about on the forward slope of the Ridge for some time, visiting a gun emplacement here and a bit of old trench there, until we came across the very thing we wanted. It was an enemy trench about twenty yards in length, shallow at either end, but deep and covered over with wood planks and earth for about eight yards in the middle so as to form an underground passage. At the beginning of the covered part at each end separate shafts with steps ran down into a splendid two-roomed dugout. It was situated about a quarter of a mile down the forward slope and the shallow trench commanded an excellent view of the enemy country for many miles. It had obviously been an officer's dugout – probably for the artillery in the gun emplacements nearby – and though not large was easily the most elaborate and comfortable dugout I ever saw. There were two rooms, the larger and lower one being connected laterally to the smaller by a flight of four steps. Each room had a separate entrance into the trench, one at either end. Both entrance shafts and both rooms were covered with boarding throughout – floors, walls and ceiling – and both rooms were neatly papered, the pattern consisting chiefly of pink roses. In the larger room were three comfortable wire-netting beds and a table and chair, and in the smaller were a mahogany table, sofa with cushions, several chairs and a large oval mirror. The smaller room was closed off from both the larger room and the trench by well-fitting doors.

After discovering this luxurious abode we went no further, but immediately pinned up notices at either end of the trench reserving it for ourselves. Then I set about making my sketch of the view while Robertson wandered in and out admiring our new premises. We had taken up with us a map, a telescope and a prismatic compass, so first of all I fixed the exact position of our new OP on the map by using back bearings from prominent landmarks, and then drew a wide kind of panoramic sketch of the whole view from it. This sketch was sent to Corps Headquarters and partially reproduced – and incidentally spoilt – by the Corps Intelligence Officer, and copies were sent to all divisions in the Third Army.

In the late afternoon we walked back over the Ridge to Roclincourt and reported on what we had done. I received instructions to take up some of the other members of the Section the next day. I took four or five of them up at 5.30 am the following morning and we remained there for two days. The weather was wet but we were perfectly comfortable in our new dugout. Our only trouble was that we ran out of cigarettes and I had to smoke 'Bird's Eye' tobacco rolled up in pages from my Field Service Message Book. On the second day it snowed and made our walk back to Roclincourt at night worse than it would have been. The top of the Ridge was in a pretty bad state at this time and the going was very heavy. Everyone had to go 'over the top' all the way for all the old enemy trenches had been blown to bits and any odd sections that remained were full of mud and water. The Ridge did not rise to a sharp edge but on the top it was a kind of tableland about a mile wide. It was this barren ground that had become so waterlogged and sodden. There were no roads over it and it was impossible to get ordinary transport across owing to the depth of mud, so everything from ammunition to rations was carried over by men or mules. The enemy always shelled when they saw any movement and we had several near misses on our journeys backwards and forwards.

The weather was very bad for the next few days and we did not go up to our OP. On the 22nd, which was a Sunday, I walked to Arras to have a look round and went into the cathedral. It was considerably damaged at this time, particularly at the east end where a shell seemed to have come through the roof onto the altar. Stones, mortar, stained glass, broken chairs etc. were all mixed up in a great heap in the chancel. The enemy began to shell it again while I was there. On the way back up the Arras–Lens road I passed close behind several of our biggest howitzers that had just been moved into position. While looking at one I failed to notice that another huge 12" was ready to fire and when it went off the roar, the enormous tongue of flame and the rush of air were all simply terrific. Some of the old dugouts by Roclincourt were now used as bomb stores and one teatime, when most of us were gathered round the field kitchen, one of the stores blew up. It was about a hundred yards from the kitchen, the ground trembled and showers of stones rattled on the corrugated iron over the fires, while men rushed for shelter from they knew not what. The tea dixies were knocked over and several gallons of boiling tea poured over the fires and streamed out on to the grass. Several horses that were picketed on the ground above the dugout store were blown up and killed. Two men were killed and one very badly burned.

On St George's Day, 23 April, the 63rd (Royal Naval) Division, who were in our Corps and on our right in the line at that time, attacked Gavrelle, a small village south of Oppy, and reports came through that they were doing very well. An attack on a wider front, including our Division, was fixed for the 28th and on the morning of the 24th I took a party of four from our Section up to the OP. I was in charge so made all the reports and – with the exception of a few hours on the 27th when I was at Divisional HQ – I remained at the OP from 24 April until 1 May, although the other men were changed twice during that period. We had a field telephone fixed in our dugout with a special wire laid direct to 'G' Office at Divisional HQ. In addition to our three ordinary telescopes we had a new and much more powerful one sent up from the base. It had three detachable lenses for use under differing atmospheric conditions and a magnification of twelve.

The weather was fine and warm the whole time and aeroplanes were up many times every day taking photographs and watching for movement behind the lines. We saw several fights almost daily and two or three came down in flames. A long string of our observation balloons ('sausages') were up a few miles behind the line. One day a very fast enemy aeroplane came racing over and set one of them on fire. In a few seconds nothing was left of it but a great cloud of black smoke. The enemy airman returned safely over his own lines while our two observers from the balloon came down by parachute into ours. These 'sausage' balloons were held captive by a steel hawser which was paid out or wound in as required. They were allowed to rise to a great height so as to get a better and more distant view, but then it was impossible to haul them in quickly enough if a fast enemy plane came over. At different times I saw five or six go up in smoke.

During the whole of this week we were watching the enemy country from daybreak until dark and often looking out for signals after dark as well. At 10.00 pm on the 25th we saw SOS rockets go up on the 63rd Divisional front on our right. We telephoned through to our 'G' officer at once and all turned out into our little trench to watch the terrific artillery barrage that very soon descended in front of the 63rd Division's line. We learnt by telephone soon afterwards that this enemy attack had been driven off successfully.

One of my instructions was to watch particularly for the passage of trains on the railway by Vitry-en-Artois along what we knew then as the 'Izel-Vitry Railway'. This was the length of the line along which troop trains were expected to bring up enemy reinforcements to our section of the front. There seemed to be some doubt as to the capacity of the railway to take many trains along this section. It was understood to be only a branch line, but one day while watching through my telescope I counted eighteen trains (or engines producing smoke at any rate) going north along the line in less than an hour. I reported this to Divisional HQ and the result was that I had visits at the OP the next morning from the Divisional Intelligence Officer, the Corps Intelligence Officer and also a major on Corps Staff. The observers at the Corps observation post had reported nothing and the point was important, because if these trains had come up full of enemy troops it would make a great difference to the big attack we were going to make a few days later. I stuck to my report and as it happened two or three more trains came up along the same section of line while the Corps major was with me and he saw them through the telescope himself. Whether these trains did bring up reinforcements of fresh troops I never heard, but our attack a few days later certainly failed and our men were driven back to their own front line trenches.

By this date (27 April) my commission papers had come through at long last and reached Divisional HQ. That morning I was sent for from the OP to go to Roclincourt to be interviewed by General Periera, the GOC 2nd Division. I saw him in his little hut and he signed my papers recommending me for a commission. In the afternoon I returned over the Ridge to the OP. Nothing now remained but to wait for instructions to proceed to England for my officer cadet course.

Zero day for the big attack was 28 April and we were up at 4.00 am with telescopes ready, waiting for the show to start. The guns had started even then and the shriek of the shells above us tearing over the Ridge together with the thunder of the explosions of the enormous howitzer shells on the enemy defences were really very cheering and encouraging to us. It made us hope for a successful show and a great advance, though their actual effect could not be seen owing to the early morning mist which still hung over the lower ground. However, it was a beautifully fine day and as the sun got through and the mists cleared we had a magnificent view of the whole battlefield from our OP. We could see all the details of the attack through our telescopes except where they were blurred by the columns and clouds of smoke from the bursting shells.

On our Divisional frontage the enemy first lines ran north and south immediately west of Oppy Wood. The Division's main objective was to capture the wood and also Oppy village itself which lay just behind it. The wood was thick and the trees tall when we first went up to the Ridge and from our position at the OP we could not see the village behind, but as the heavy shelling continued day after day the trees got very considerably thinned out so that by the morning of the attack parts of some of the buildings could be discerned through occasional gaps in the now blackened, leafless wood. The 6th Brigade of the 2nd Division led the attack and made good progress at first advancing right through the wood and into Oppy village. However, owing to the failure of the 63rd Division on the right, their flank was left exposed and they were obliged to retire and were back again in our old front line by the afternoon. It was months later before Oppy village was again occupied by our troops.

In addition to the flanking fire our troops had been very seriously harassed by enemy machine guns in some of the buildings in the village, so in the afternoon it was decided to shell Oppy with our heaviest howitzers. We received this information by telephone from Divisional HQ and were instructed to watch the bombardment and report. About twenty minutes after our telephone call we heard the first of the great 12" shells 'wobbling' over. There was a pause as the height of the trajectory caused the shell to get out of range of our hearing, then we heard the 'wobble' again as the shell came down, followed by a most terrific rumbling roar and an eruption of black smoke mixed with red brick dust as part of the village went up in the air. After that, crash followed crash for about half an hour as column after column of smoke and red dust rose and hung like a pall over the ruined village. Oppy must have been built principally of brick for after every shell a great cloud of red dust shot up far above the tops of the highest trees in the wood and mingled with the great black cloud of slowly rolling, curling smoke that gradually drifted away south. For two days after that (29 and 30 April) we remained at the OP while attack followed attack and counter-attack followed counter-attack, but all without appreciable gain or loss of ground although the casualties were terrible.

At about 6 o'clock one evening I noticed a big, heavy, tired-looking soldier with rifle slung slowly trudging up the Ridge behind three young washed-out German prisoners. I thought I seemed to recognize his build and on turning the telescope on to him I found it was Spud Taylor of D Company, the 24th Royal Fusiliers. I ran along to the track he was following to have a word with him. I found him perspiring copiously and swearing horribly at the heat, the hill and the war generally. Like all men from the front line he knew little or nothing of how the attack was going except on his own immediate front, but he said it was hell in the valley and that the 24th had had many casualties. That was the last time I saw him and he passed over the Ridge with his prisoners profanely eloquent to the last.

On the afternoon of the 28th, after our troops had retired from Oppy village, we were most surprised to see a long string of enemy motor lorries advancing along the main Vitry–Arras road towards their front line. We informed Divisional HQ at once over the telephone but were told that the artillery had orders not to shell that road as it would ultimately be one of the main routes of advance for our heavy transport and guns, so we did not want the road surface to be damaged. The lorries came forward to a point perhaps three-quarters of a mile from the front line and there each set down about twenty-eight men who ran forward across the open for some distance and then jumped down into one of their reserve trenches. Later the same day the enemy put up a large Red Cross flag in their front line and after a short interval a man came out onto the top waving this flag, while stretcher bearers hurriedly collected the wounded who were lying out in No Man's Land exposed to the hot afternoon sun. After about half an hour they returned to their trench and the flag was taken in.

By the 29th the Division on our left had captured the village of Arleux, north of Oppy, and our front line now sloped back from there along 'Arleux switch trench' to the north corner of Oppy Wood. During the afternoon of that day the enemy launched a big attack across the open in extended order against this line just north of the wood. It was a hot sunny afternoon and the whole front seemed quiet for the moment, when suddenly we saw in the distance wave after wave of enemy troops come forward from the outskirts of Neuvireuil (a village a mile east of Oppy) and advance steadily towards our new line. We telephoned Divisional HQ once more and after an enquiry they informed us that the artillery observers had seen the enemy movements: all the available guns were being trained on a barrage line a little farther forward and they would wait until the enemy reached it.

We therefore hurried back from the telephone to the trench and picked up our telescopes to watch the show. The enemy was still advancing and the rear waves were now closing up more on the front ones and massing for the attack, but still our artillery was silent. Then, as the attackers came within sight of our front-line troops, we heard a rising rattle of machine-guns all along the line and a few seconds later, but without the slightest warning, our artillery barrage fell on them like a tornado. Shrapnel screamed and hissed over them, HE (high explosive) crashed and 'crumped' amongst them and in a few moments a dense curtain of smoke shut them out from view. After perhaps three minutes of intense fire our barrage lifted and as the smoke cleared we saw that the massed lines had been swept away, while odd survivors here and there were running as fast as they possibly could back to the shelter of Neuvireuil.

May

Early on the morning of 1 May I left the OP for the last time. I returned to Roclincourt and reported at the 5th Field Ambulance for a last medical inspection. After I had safely passed this my commissioning papers were complete. As it happened a small party of men who were waiting for commissions were due to leave the Division the next day. As one of them had been killed the day before, the Staff Sergeant at '2' Office, who was a friend of mine, put me down in his place. The Staff Sergeant himself was going to Aubigny early the next morning in the GOC's Rolls Royce to collect some special stores, so I got up at 4.30 am and went with him, picking up my train to Boulogne from there at about noon. One of the hotels on the front near the harbour at Boulogne was reserved for men going home for commissions and I had a good night there on a real bedstead – the first for almost a year.

At 11.00 am on 3 May I landed at Folkestone. I had seen it last on 12 May 1916. I reported at 38 Parliament Street, London, in the afternoon and was sent on to the Royal Fusiliers Depot at Hounslow for the night. The next morning I drew £7 at the Pay Office and got some new kit. With a warrant for a month's furlough in my pocket I left Hounslow in the afternoon and reached Sheffield at 8.32 pm. Home once more.

June, England

I had a good holiday and rest from 4 May until 3 June when I returned to Hounslow Barracks. I remained there for eight days, going for short marches on several mornings but being off most afternoons. One day I was on the Air Raid Picket and another day on Regimental Guard. While on guard we had four conscientious objectors in the cells when the reports and sentences of their courts martial were read out. They received 112 days' hard labour each. Another day I was one of a party who went to Northwood (beyond Harrow) as bearers and firing party at a military funeral. It was a long journey across London by train to Northwood and we had a long 'slow march' from the house to the church, and then on to the cemetery. Altogether it was a rather depressing day.

On 12 June about thirty other men and I who were home for commissions were transferred from Hounslow to Aldershot. We were billeted in Talaxua Barracks, Wellington Lines (just on the edge of the town). We were all made lance corporals (except those who were NCOs already) and our duties were to go on parade with the boys in one of the training battalions and to help with their instruction. We had a pretty easy time – no fatigues or guards – though two or three times we went out with the boys at night on practice 'night operations'. On 30 June a number of us were posted to Officer Cadet Battalions (in my case No. 4 Platoon B Company, 6th OCB). Ramsden and I were down for Balliol College, Oxford.

July–October, Oxford

We went on leave from Aldershot at once and after a few days at home I reported to Balliol College on 5 July. I met Ramsden at the station in Sheffield on the way down and when we reached Oxford we found that we were both to be billeted at Trinity College. Four of us – Wolfenden, Cooper, Ramsden and myself – shared a good-sized room looking on to the Quadrangle and The Broad. At one time it was Quiller-Couch's room. We soon settled down at Oxford and had a really good time during our four months' course. We worked hard but had some good times on the tennis courts and on the river. We used to bathe early in the morning at 'Parson's Pleasure', have various parades both morning and afternoon, and then two hours' 'prep' at night from eight to ten. We had half holidays on Wednesdays and Saturdays after the CO's weekly parade and inspection in the park.

On 4 August, Mother and Father came to Oxford for the weekend and stayed at the Clarendon Hotel. On 21 August we were inspected by Sir William Robertson, Chief of the General Staff. We had examinations every month and on 30 October we had our final War Office examination. I got 207 marks out of a possible 290 and so passed comfortably. The top man got 226 and I was third. I left Oxford on the afternoon of the 31st and reached home the same night.

November–December

I had just over three weeks' leave this time and was then gazetted a Second Lieutenant in the West Yorkshire Regiment and ordered to report to the Headquarters of the 3rd Battalion at Whitley Bay on 24 November. Ramsden was gazetted to the same Regiment and I met him again on the way up. We were billeted together at Belle Vue House, East Parade, a boarding house on the front. We were attached to No. 6 Company while we were there and attended the usual parades of the depot men. We could not get Christmas leave and so spent Christmas Day at Whitley Bay. On 26 December orders were issued for a number of us to go to Rugeley on the 28th to be attached to the West

Riding Regiment (Duke of Wellington's) 6th Reserve Battalion. We were at Rugeley (Cannock Chase) for only a few days before both Ramsden and I were sent off on 'Draft Leave' on 31 December, with instructions to report at Folkestone on 11 January 1918 for service overseas once again.

1918

January

Early on the morning of 11 January I boarded the troop train at Victoria Station, got a seat in the Pullman reserved for officers, and in due course crossed the Channel and arrived at Étaples. After waiting there for two days both Ramsden and I were posted to the 10th (Service) Battalion of the West Yorkshire Regiment, which at that time was in the trenches in front of Havrincourt in the Cambrai salient. We left Étaples by train in the morning and arrived at Rocquigny – the railhead for the Havrincourt area – a little after midnight. After a short rest in a hut we left our valises to be collected by the transport and walked to Bertincourt where we found B Echelon (transport etc.) of the 10th Battalion.

We introduced ourselves to Lieutenant Jamieson (the acting Lieutenant Quartermaster) and Second Lieutenant S.H.B. Gill (the Transport Officer), and arranged for our kit to be sent for. Lieutenant Jamieson was a nervous and excitable sort of man who had a servant called Cass. He seemed to spend most of his time putting his head round the hut door and shouting 'Cass, Cass' in a high, irritable voice. He was in bad health at the time and left the Battalion soon afterwards. Second Lieutenant Gill was a solicitor by profession and came from Wakefield. He was a tall, broad young man, already inclined to put on weight, which he

112

afterwards did to a considerable extent. The transport took the Battalion rations up to the line that night as usual and brought back instructions that Ramsden and I were to go up to Battalion HQ the following night.

The next morning I chose my first servant (batman) who was a married man called Wilkinson. He proved to be a good careful servant who remained with me until he was wounded in the front line on 21 March. In the evening we set off with the transport, passing through the remains of Ruyaulcourt, along the road made of wooden 'sleepers' through Havrincourt Wood, down 'Pioneer Valley', up the slope near the 'Spoil Heap', past the 'Soup Kitchen', through Havrincourt village (this last at a gallop as it was a dangerous spot) and so on to the reserve trench where the Battalion HQ dugout was situated. It was then about 11.00 pm and very dark but fine.

The transport men dumped their rations by the trench side while Gill gave one or two messages he had brought and then off they went as fast as possible back to Bertincourt, leaving us to meet the CO – Lieutenant Colonel P.R.O. Simner DSO. He was a tall, spare, very precise man (a barrister by profession) who loved to hear himself pronounce judgement on anything and everything in a very learned, judicial way; nevertheless he was very brave, fair-minded and essentially honourable. I always got on with him very well indeed. All the men of the Battalion respected him and I think the reason was that they knew they could always expect a fair hearing and a calm, unbiased judgement. He decided that Ramsden should be attached to B Company at once and join them in the line, while I should go to the Brigade School for a short course on 'Wiring'.

Fourteen men and one officer were to go on the course. As the men had already been detailed and were waiting at Battalion HQ, I was instructed to take them back to B Echelon that night and report to the Brigade School the next day. These men had been in the line for some days and were tired and plastered with mud. They were all more or less ill and unfit: I believe they had been chosen for the course more because of the respite from trench miseries it would afford them than because of the experience in wiring they would gain. It was a long, weary trail for them back to Bertincourt and I was relieved when we arrived safely at about 4.00 am. Even so I had to beg lifts on a lorry for two who collapsed by the roadside near Ruyaulcourt.

I joined the Brigade School in the afternoon, taking my servant and kit with me. I found a small but jolly party of officers there: Second Lieutenants Hancocks and Franzini were the instructors in wiring, and Lieutenant M.F. Smith (afterwards Captain of D Company, 10th West Yorks) was the instructor in bombing. I found out at once that it was not a school for officers at all – there had been a mistake somewhere – but they had a spare bed in their hut so I made myself comfortable and settled down for a nice quiet week. There were about forty men on the course and every morning I went out with Hancocks and helped to teach the men different methods of wiring. Every afternoon we had about an hour more of the same thing before we finished for the day.

Hancocks was the Mess President and one evening he arranged a very nice little dinner to which were invited Doctor Abrahams from the Brigade Rest Camp nearby and Captain Green of the East Yorkshires, the Lieutenant Quartermaster, both of whom were with us in 50 Brigade, 17th Division. There were the six of us when we sat down to dinner although only three remained until the end. The orchestra from the Band of the 10th West Yorkshires had been borrowed for the evening and were fixed up for the occasion in the bedroom part of the hut which was shut off by a wooden partition from the Mess where the dinner was held. The orchestra played excellently, the cooks had cooked excellently and Hancocks had provided excellently, in fact profusely, in the way of drinks. Franzini was strictly teetotal and stuck to soda water throughout the evening. Even so, when Hancocks counted up the empty bottles the next morning, he found we had accounted for three bottles of port, two of sherry, seven of whisky and twenty-three of soda water. Altogether we had a very merry time. The orchestra left at about 10.30 pm and about an hour later Hancocks suddenly gave up the running and retired to bed. Soon after midnight Smith had had enough and with difficulty reached his bed in the next room. I followed him a little later. We heard the next morning that the remainder of the party broke up at about 1.45 am after spending about a quarter of an hour in getting Captain Green onto his horse en route for the East Yorkshire's transport lines.

During the week I was at the Brigade School, enemy bombing planes came over on several nights. One aeroplane passed almost directly over us at about seven o'clock on the night of the dinner and dropped several large bombs in the district. It was surprising to watch some of the lame men from the Brigade Rest Camp (suffering from trench feet) running to the shelter of the practice bombing trenches near our hut. One bomb dropped on the Orderly Room of the East Yorkshires and knocked the hut to pieces, scattering papers and records of various kinds in all directions. A deserter awaiting trial by court martial was imprisoned in the guard room hut at the time and the hut collapsed when the bomb exploded and he made his escape. He was not recaptured until about a fortnight later when attempting to board the leave boat at Boulogne.

At the end of my week of 'wiring' I returned to B Echelon and from there rejoined the Battalion which had moved back from the trenches into dugouts in Hermies village. I was attached to D Company and there met 'Ginger' Newton who was in command at the time. I happened to mention to him that I had been on Intelligence work with the 2nd Division previous to getting my commission and he at once suggested that I should take over the work of the Intelligence Officer,

Captain A.T. Brown, who was then on leave. The CO
(Lieutenant Colonel Simner) was away on a short visit to
one of the RFC squadrons, but on his return to the Battalion
the next day he agreed to the suggestion and I transferred
myself from D Company to Battalion Headquarters.

On the very day on which I took over this appointment
orders came through from Brigade giving the positions the
Battalion was to occupy during the next tour in the line. In
checking over these instructions with the aid of trench maps
and aeroplane photographs, it appeared to me that we were
ordered to occupy ground which was in fact in the possession of the enemy and behind his front line. I pointed this out
to the CO but he did not agree and said he thought I was
mistaken. However, after going over it all again by myself I
was quite convinced I was right, so I asked him to look at
the maps once more, finally proving to him that the Brigade
instructions were wrong and that we could not possibly take
over the positions indicated unless we first captured them
from the enemy. The Brigade Staff were always very ready to
point out sarcastically any mistakes made by the Battalion,
so when the CO realized that the Brigade had made a slip he
was delighted and spent a pleasant half hour composing an
ironical request for instructions as to how we were to take
over a position behind the enemy lines. Incidentally, my map
reading abilities went up in his estimation.

On one afternoon during our stay in the Hermies dugouts
we were very heavily shelled with gas. All the men were
instructed to wear their respirators but it was always
difficult to make them keep them on for long, especially as
the gas used did not smell much and everything seemed
clear. On this occasion a number of men took off their
respirators too soon and, though they felt no ill effects at the
time, the next morning several of them were temporarily
blind; altogether we had twenty casualties. Two nights later
we took over the section of the line immediately west of the
Canal du Nord. Our stay of six days was fairly quiet but I

had my first experience of an Intelligence Officer's duties in the line. I soon found that, though interesting, they were practically endless. Three hours sleep out of the twenty-four was the most I ever expected and sometimes I got less.

February

I had a small Observation Section of four men and an NCO, and I also formed a Sniping Section which eventually consisted of eight men with two NCOs. The Observation Section sent me their reports every day at 3.00 am and 3.00 pm, and all company commanders also sent me their 'Situation' and 'Direction of Wind' reports at about the same times. All these reports had to be edited and forwarded to Brigade by 4.00 am and 4.00 pm each day, together with scaled-down maps showing the position of each unit. 'Work reports' of trenches dug, cleaned and repaired, wiring of trenches done, dugouts made, machine-gun emplacements prepared etc. were also sent to me periodically by companies, to be edited, combined into one report and forwarded to Brigade. The reports required at 4.00 am were the ones appreciated least. To get up in a cold dark dugout at about 3.00 am and when only half awake, to have to write out reports, draw plans and check map references by the light of a candle is a very uncomfortable and uninspiring business, even when fortified by half a cup of Army rum. I had also to arrange for and inform Brigade of all men who were casualties or ordered to go on instructional courses. I was PMC of the Battalion HQ Mess and had to order all special rations and drinks from the canteens and keep all the accounts.

I accompanied the CO each night on his midnight tour of the front line and interviewed all gunner officers, trench mortar officers and others who wanted information or instructions. In spare moments I censored all the HQ men's letters. I was responsible for all the maps issued to Battalion by Brigade and distributed them to company commanders and others as required. The accumulation of these maps of different areas, sizes and scales, together with 'trench maps', plans, panoramic views, aeroplane photographs and the like was simply amazing. Later on, in May 1918, when I had time to overhaul the stock carried by the transport, we had five large wooden crates full, sufficient to fill a half limber in addition to those actually in use by the Battalion officers at the time. In connection with my PMC duties I often received requests from company commanders for bottles of whisky etc. pending the arrival of their next supplies. One such request from Captain Burne, then in command of D Company, ran as follows: 'Dear Spencer, This war cannot go on unless D Company have a drink. Some ordered from B Echelon but not arrived yet. Could you spare a bottle until tomorrow? Yours etc. W.L. Burne.'

The relief of one Battalion by another in the line was always a tiring and tedious business, made worse in winter by the pitch darkness of the nights and the normal presence of mud and water. Guides were usually sent down to some rendezvous behind the reserve line by the outgoing Battalion and these led the various companies and HQ personnel up to their new positions. Trench stores were then handed over and signed for, the peculiarities of particular positions explained, and the requirements of the work in progress stated until at last the outgoing units moved off towards the rear, leaving the fresh Battalion to take stock of their surroundings and settle down as best they could to the routine of trench life.

When we arrived at our Battalion HQ in the reserve line on this occasion, we found that an Artillery Observation Officer was quartered with us in the same dugout. On the first morning after our arrival I went round the line with him calling at all Company Headquarters and introducing him to the company commanders. His business was to find suitable

targets for his battery and he asked all company commanders to inform him of the positions of any enemy
machine-guns, trench mortar batteries etc. that were
troubling them during the nights, so that he could train his
guns on them during the day and perhaps knock them out of
action. It was really a rather jolly sort of holiday for me to
get away from the HQ dugout and go round with him on
fine mornings. We had a chat and a drink at each Company
HQ and heard all the news, although every now and then we
had to move rather hurriedly when any shelling began. One
day we reached D Company HQ just after a shell had blown
in the dugout entrance and on another occasion we were
close to 'Betty' and 'Babs' posts in the front line when the
parapet was blown in. On another day we were returning to
Battalion HQ when a large shell crashed down a few feet
outside the trench and a large piece which had been blown
high in the air came down directly onto my steel helmet. It
did not penetrate it but made a fair-sized dent and I had a
stiff neck for several days. If this had happened to me in
1915 or 1916 before we were supplied with steel helmets, I
might well have been killed.

Nothing of importance happened for the next two or three
weeks and by then the Intelligence Officer (Captain Brown)
had returned from leave, so I left Battalion HQ and joined D
Company. The next time in the line after his return A
Company held the firing line on the east side of the Canal du
Nord and as they were short of officers I was transferred to
them temporarily. We were in the old Hindenburg Line and
Company HQ was at one end of a long wide tunnel, perhaps
sixty yards long, that ran under a little ridge of high ground
and connected one section of the line with another. Nearby
were the shattered remains of three tanks that had been put
out of action at some time during the capture of the trenches.

The enemy were quite a long way off in front of the village
of Graincourt. Some distance out in No Man's Land was a
rather large old 'strongpoint' known as 'Reindeer Post'.

On the second night in the line I was ordered to take a patrol of ten men out past Reindeer Post, which was reported to be unoccupied, push on towards the enemy trenches and try to obtain identification. That is to say I was to try to capture some of the enemy or otherwise to find out what regiment was opposed to us. I knew none of the men of A Company or which ones might be suitable for a patrol of this kind, but after very considerable difficulty I collected eight most unwilling men and set out across No Man's Land in the direction of Reindeer Post.

My intention was to examine the Post first and then to advance carefully on the enemy trenches. We walked upright across our own belt of barbed wire and were within perhaps seventy yards of the Post when we were met by a blaze of rifle fire from the Post itself. Bullets hissed round us and we hastily flung ourselves full length. After a few minutes we crept forward a little farther and fired a few rounds in the direction of the Post which was in low ground. We could see nothing, although they could evidently see us on the ridge and dropped three or four Very lights right amongst us. It would have been quite hopeless and futile to attack the Post with my men and equally so to go past its flank and leave the enemy in my rear, so I finally decided that the only thing to do was to return and report the Post occupied. This I did and dismissed the men with the exception of one lance corporal who was a much more suitable man for patrol work than any of the others. Because the patrol proper had had such an inglorious ending I went out again with him alone to see if anything more could be done. As soon as we got over the edge of the slight ridge they spotted us and fired again, so after a few unsuccessful attempts to light up their position with the aid of a Very pistol we returned to our front line for the remainder of the night.

Two nights later Lieutenant Braithwaite with twelve specially picked men, supported by a Lewis gun and team posted well out in No Man's Land on the flank, crept out to

Reindeer Post at dusk and occupied it before the arrival of the enemy garrison who came out well after dark. In the short fight that ensued several of the enemy were believed to have been hit, while our party had one man killed and two wounded, but were driven out of the Post soon afterwards by heavy trench mortar fire, and forced to return to our own trenches without having obtained any identifications. Some time previous to this I had put in an application for transfer to the Kite Balloon Observation Section of the RFC. I obtained an excellent recommendation from Colonel Simner but was eventually refused, apparently on medical grounds. No exact reason was stated but on my application sheet the medical report was queried. (It was not very enthusiastic.) However I was able to get one interesting day out of the matter for on about 20 February I was ordered to report at Amiens for an interview. I got there during the morning and managed to see a good deal of the town before I made my way to the Officers' Club in the early evening for dinner and a room for the night. I went into the cathedral and saw the enormous amount of sandbagging and barricading that had been done to protect it. The valuable stained glass from some of the large windows had been removed altogether to a place of safety. Apart from this the town seemed very busy and normal, trams were running in the streets, motor cars were numerous, all the shops were open as usual and the only noticeable signs of the war were the state of the cathedral and the number of men in uniform. The cafés and estaminets were very busy and I went to the famous 'Charlie's Bar' and sampled one or two of the drinks. On the following day I returned – partly by train – to the Battalion and rejoined D Company.

I remained with D Company from this time forward until after the great German attack on 21 March 1918. The 17th Division as a whole was not relieved until the end of March and we of the 10th West Yorkshires never got further back than close reserve positions round about

Havrincourt village and the 'Mortar Valley Spoil Heap', which was a huge oblong 'hill' made from the pre-war excavation of the partially completed Canal du Nord. The bed of the Canal was dry and was used by troops and transport as a road for relief and rationing purposes. It was frequently shelled and was exposed to enemy machine-gun fire where it cut through the front line beyond 'Lock 7'. Its sides were very steep and it was about thirty feet deep and lined with brick. Immediately to the south of the Spoil Heap was a slope of open furze-covered ground called 'Cheetham Hill High Woods', where the remnants of old trenches remained and where a few fairly deep dugouts were situated. One of these dugouts was used as our Company HQ when we were in reserve. It had two entrances until one day while we were there a shell hit one of the entrances and completely knocked it in. After that we were careful to keep a pick and spade inside so that if the other entrance was hit we might be able to dig ourselves out.

Several of us were in this dugout one evening and I was lying reading on an upper wire bed with Captain Billy Burne on the lower one beneath me. I had hung up my revolver ammunition pouch on a nail and had a lighted candle stuck on the bed frame by which to read. The light was in a rather inconvenient position so I moved the candle a few inches to get a better light on my paper. A few minutes later there was a loud explosion and revolver bullets and cartridge cases went flying all round the dugout, several of them missing Burne and me by inches. When the commotion subsided I found that my revolver ammunition had all gone off and that my pouch was torn to ribbons. I had inadvertently moved the candle to a position just below the pouch and the heat from the flame had done the rest. Fortunately no one was hurt. Captain Burne had a famous recipe for making what he called rum punch. It was a concoction of army rum, Ideal milk and sugar, all heated together. It was an extraordinarily powerful mixture and taking two or three table-spoonfuls of it one night Second Lieutenant Gibson (Gibbie) began to laugh at some feeble joke and could not stop for about an hour. In the end we had to threaten to throw him outside.

March

About this time (the end of February and beginning of March) it became very evident that a big enemy offensive was expected. An enormous amount of work had been done in improving our forward defences during the previous two months and the position on the divisional front was really strong, but it was not the development of the first trench system that attracted attention and provoked discussion, rather the elaborate preparations that were being made to defend areas miles behind the front line.

Cheetham Hill High Woods (the north-west section of Havrincourt Wood), where our reserve dugout was situated, was nearly 3 miles as the crow flies from the front line and a number of heavy howitzers were in position there, but all these big gun emplacements were wired round for protection against infantry attack; each gun team was supplied with and trained in the use of Lewis machine guns and also Mills bombs. It was evidently expected that the enemy attack might penetrate the front system with such speed that the guns could not be withdrawn and that the gun teams should fire their guns to the last moment and continue to defend them at the closest quarters.

In many and various other ways information and rumours trickled through to the front-line battalions about the over-whelming weight of the expected attack and the most exceptional preparations that were being made to withstand it. Men returning from leave brought rumours of leave being stopped, men from hospital of all hospitals being rapidly cleared, men from instructional courses of trench systems being dug, large ammunition dumps formed and gun emplacements fixed many miles behind the lines. Then the Brigade, Divisional and Corps Intelligence reports began to refer to the numbers of enemy divisions and formations being concentrated on our immediate front and the great numbers and size of enemy dumps of food, ammunition and materials spotted by our aeroplanes. Finally we received definite official information about the great expected offensive and orders for our defence.

The date fixed by the enemy was probably the 13th but certainly not later than 21 March. Tanks might possibly be used by them and all troops were to keep a constant lookout for any moving objects behind the enemy lines that resembled tanks or armoured cars. Drawings of a new enemy tank were forwarded to battalions. Patrols were to be out in No Man's Land every night on the lookout for concentrations of enemy troops. All Lewis guns were to fire through our own wire intermittently every night, particularly just before daybreak. All circulars, company papers, and correspondence of all kinds in the possession of companies in the line were to be destroyed. Plentiful supplies of rifle ammunition and bombs were to be obtained and examined ready for instant use. All iron rations and gas respirators were to be inspected and reported in order. Finally all troops were expected to stand to their positions and never retreat.

On about 10 March Colonel Simner came round the front line to give his last instructions and say goodbye to the Company officers. I was with D Company in the front line and that night Captain Burne, who was in command, destroyed all the Company papers and made his will. As may be imagined the situation was tense. Everyone was braced for the apparently inevitable finale. The attack was expected to take place on the 13th and D Company was not to be relieved but would be holding the front line that morning. In an offensive of such magnitude, where troops miles back were hardly hoping to retain their positions, it seemed beyond belief that any of us would survive the day. But our suspense was not to be over so soon. The 13th came but there was no attack and it was not until the early hours of the 21st that lining the same parapet once more, the long awaited barrage descended on us and we 'stood to' to meet the advancing waves of men.

It may be as well to describe here the sector of line we held and had to defend on 21 March. It was about 400 yards long and was in an extremely dilapidated condition. It had been the scene of very heavy fighting during the previous autumn and had been shelled to such an extent that most of it was merely a kind of shattered, debris-strewn lane, so wide in many places that a pony and cart could have been driven down it and so wrecked that no firing steps remained. In some parts the accumulation of blown-in parapet and parados made it too shallow to allow standing upright in daytime. Here and there it was under water and almost everywhere thick with mud except for about 100 yards on the left flank. It had been a German trench originally and the one and only dugout faced the wrong way, that is, it was dug down into the parados so that the open entrance faced the enemy lines. The left (west) section of the trench was narrow, fairly new and ended with a sheer drop of about thirty feet into the Canal du Nord.

At this time the fighting strength of D Company was only about fifty bayonets and it was quite impossible for them to man the whole of such a long, rambling, shattered frontage; so six widely separated posts, which had been more or less repaired, were held by small garrisons of six to eight men each. Four of these were Lewis gun posts and in addition our fifth (Company HQ) Lewis gun team was posted in a fire bay close to the Company Headquarters dugout on the right (east) flank of the company frontage. There was only one communication trench leading to the support line and it ran back from the front line at a point about 100 yards from our right flank. Such was our line of defence on 21 March – six small, practically isolated posts on a frontage of nearly a quarter of a mile. Even these were merely patched-up fire bays, quite open and unprotected against attack from the flanks or rear. It seemed a thin, pitiably weak defence with which to attempt to hold up, even for an hour, the most terrific attack in the greatest war in history. Yet it stood firm that first day under the most murderous, overwhelming barrages of poison gas and high explosive, and then flung back and completely routed a frontal attack by more than 300 of the enemy.

On the night of 10/11 March I took out a small patrol of five or six men to see if there was any enemy activity in No Man's Land. We remained out for more than an hour but nothing happened and all seemed quiet. On the afternoon of 12 March our gas experts in the rear fired 22 tons of gas from special projectors into the enemy lines. Before this was done the left half of our Company was retired from the three posts nearest the canal and ordered into a large dugout in the support line where I was placed in charge of them. Respirators were worn the whole time. The gas cylinders were fired electrically and made no sound, but clouds of gas could be seen over the enemy trenches and in the low ground generally near the canal. In the early evening the men returned to their posts in the front line after the gas corporal had reported the trench free from gas. However, it soon appeared that some gas had blown back and still hung about the area; about half a dozen of our men were slightly gassed and felt rather sick, though they recovered by the following morning.

At about 2.00 am on the morning of the 13th our artillery put down a terrific barrage which lasted until dawn and made certain that no enemy attack would be forthcoming. Shells of all calibres swept over No Man's Land and reached back into the enemy support and reserve lines. The continuous explosions lighted up their trenches and blew their wire to pieces. All our patrols were brought in; shell splinters and nose caps frequently came hissing and screaming back towards our own line. On the 14th we were relieved by the 7th East Yorkshires and went back to the reserve positions near the Spoil Heap for four days. On the 18th we should have been relieved by another Division but the attack was then so imminent that the relief was cancelled. We returned to the front area and the East Yorkshires came back into close reserve. B Company went into the front line on the right of the canal with D Company in the support trenches behind them, but on the evening of the 20th we exchanged positions and so it came about that D Company held the front line on the following and most eventful morning.

On the night of 18/19 I took out a party of five men at midnight and patrolled the whole of the Company front from Company HQ on the right to the canal bank on the left and back again. Everything was fairly quiet and we were out for more than two hours. We moved in the usual arrowhead formation with myself at the point and two men spread out behind on either side, while the fifth was well back in the centre as a rear guard. Patrolling is rather nerve-wracking work: out in No Man's Land everything seems so strangely hushed and still. The slightest sound one makes seems to ring out as if all the world must hear it. Small bushes and mounds of earth loom black and large, and shadows seem to move about. Everything looks different and mysterious in the dark. The light plays tricks and lighter patches seem to come and go. Ground mist creeps up and curls into fantastic shapes. We crawl a few yards stealthily on hands and knees, revolver or rifle in hand, peering through the darkness, straining our eyes and ears for the slightest sign of life. After going a short distance we stop, lie down full length and listen again. No one speaks a whisper, not a sound is heard. When everything seems clear we stand up and move on again, keeping to our arrow formation, looking in every direction, listening for the slightest sound. Sooner or later there is a distant 'puff' and a Very light shoots up from the enemy trenches; instantly everyone stops and stands quite still; whether it drops near or far we remain like statues, immovable until the last spark dies away. Perhaps an enemy machine-gun opens fire, traversing along its 'night lines' on our parapet; immediately every man flings himself full length in the grass and remains there until all is quiet once more. So we go on a few yards at a time, every man supremely watchful and alert, keyed up for anything, suspicious of all.

On this particular occasion we moved slowly across our front a short distance outside our own wire, keeping the keenest lookout but seeing nothing of enemy parties or patrols. With the exception of the usual occasional Very lights or short bursts of machine-gun fire all was quiet. Whenever we came to any slight rise or ridge in the ground I went ahead first. If I found it clear on the other side, I signalled to the remainder of the patrol to follow one at a time and quickly, so as to show up for as short a time as possible to any enemy patrol that might be lying in lower ground. We had already crossed one raised road and the remains of a light railway line in this way when we came to another slightly raised piece of ground that looked like a second road. I signalled to the others to wait until I got across, then quickly scrambled up the bank and across the level top. I was on the point of descending on the other side when I noticed that it was an exceptionally steep and sudden drop into the darkness and realized that I was on the extreme edge of the canal. Another foot forward and I would have found myself on the canal bottom thirty feet below. It is extremely difficult to judge distance in the dark and I had not realized we had come so far. I crawled back to the others and told them where we were.

We had probably been seen by our own post close to the canal bank so I walked up to our wire to give them our password and tell them all was well. When a patrol went out the front-line posts were always informed of it, given the password for the night and instructed not to fire. I stepped forward gingerly amongst the outer fringe of tangled wire and when I heard them challenge gave our password 'Splendid' in a loud stage whisper. I could see their bayonets gleaming over the parapet and heard them whisper together. Then they challenged again 'Who goes there?' Again I gave the password 'Splendid', louder still this time. They did not seem to understand; once more I was challenged and replied. Then the line of rifles levelled, safety catches clicked back and a voice called, 'Say who you are or we fire.' I almost hissed at them, 'West Yorkshire, you fools.' I was only just in time. I was standing up covered by them all and the sergeant in charge of the post told me afterwards that in another second they would have fired. It transpired that whilst being whispered from man to man and carried on from post to post, our password had become altered into another word altogether so that the men in the end post did not recognize my answer.

THE GERMAN OFFENSIVE

When the morning of the 21st came we were as well prepared as could be in such a poorly fortified position. We had plenty of rifle ammunition and Mills bombs. At my suggestion each of the five Lewis gun teams had taken out a thousand rounds of ammunition from bandoliers and rifle clips and put them in a box by the gun so as to be able to reload their drums with the minimum delay. The direction and area of fire of each gun had been carefully planned out by Ramsden, then the Battalion Machine-Gun Officer, so that the whole of our front was covered by crossfire from one gun or another. No gun fired to its immediate front but laterally so that No Man's Land would be swept from end to end. Captain Burne had left D Company a few days before and we were commanded by Captain A.N.L. Clarke who remained in the support firing line so that the officers in the front line were Sydney Lowden, 'Babs' Ramsden and myself.

The enemy bombardment commenced at a little before 5.00 am and before it was properly light. It consisted entirely of trench mortar bombs of all calibres as far as the front line was concerned, and at first was mainly gas rather than high explosive. It very soon reached a simply terrific intensity with light, medium and huge 'minenwerfer' trench mortar bombs raining down on us on every side, filling the trench with thick heavy gas, compelling us to put on our gas respirators at once. Everyone felt sure that the great attack was coming at last, but there was no confusion and every man stood to his post and waited in readiness for whatever should happen next.

As it became light a fairly thick white mist lay over No Man's Land. In the trench itself the smoke and gas from the incessant deluge of trench mortar bombs, coupled with the condensation of moisture in the goggles of our respirators, made it impossible to see for more than a few feet ahead. We had to grope along with hands outstretched as we went backwards and forwards from post to post, encouraging the men and making sure once more that all were ready and prepared. It spoke well for our respirators and our recent careful test of them that not a man was seriously affected by gas throughout this dense and deadly bombardment which lasted for two hours until about 7 o'clock.

We partly removed our respirators for a few seconds from time to time to find out if the gas was still as thick as ever. A little after 7 o'clock it appeared to be clearing away, although the barrage generally seemed more severe than before. This was because those batteries that had been firing gas, which makes little noise on bursting, had now changed over to high explosive, which crashed and thundered as it fell, so that the trench seemed to shudder as pieces of earth broke off and fell from the sides and parados into the bottom to add to those that showered in every few moments directly from the bursts themselves. We had to shout to make ourselves heard above the din and the rolling smoke now took the place of the morning mist which gradually cleared away.

We had two signallers with their telephones in the Company dugout and at first we could get our messages through to Battalion HQ and B Company in support, but before long all their lines had gone and we were cut off from everyone beyond our own front trench. The smoke made it impossible for us to see anything of our support line on the higher ground behind and it seemed hopeless to expect a runner to get through alive. We simply stood and waited. Probably very few of us would have survived that endless hail of shells, but by the most amazing good fortune the enemy had made their range just a little long so that most of the shells passed over us and tore up the ground behind. Nine o'clock came and still the bombardment continued. The men crouched in the bottom of the trench or on the fire step by their Lewis guns. No. 16 Platoon gun was blown from its position into the trench and one or two of the team slightly wounded; farther down the line one of the sergeants was killed.

At about this time 'Babs' Ramsden, a man of the Company HQ Lewis gun team and I were standing close together in a traverse near the gun when a trench mortar bomb burst with a great flash and roar immediately behind us on the parados. I was not hit but a small piece passed through Ramsden's cheek and out through his mouth. The Lewis gunner got a large piece in the back which came out through his chest. He sank slowly to the ground and died immediately without a word. We carried him to the dugout and laid him on the steps a few feet down the shaft. The trench had to be kept clear and there was nowhere else. After this I told Ramsden it seemed useless to remain there doing nothing but waiting to be killed; we should be wanted later when the actual attack began and in the meantime we might rest ourselves and get some food. We had had nothing since the evening before and I was hungry, so we went down into the Company dugout and ordered breakfast.

The time was about 9.40 am, we had had some porridge and were waiting for the bacon and tomatoes that the Company cook was frying on a brazier at the bottom of the steps, when we heard a wild yell from up in the trench: 'They're coming over, they're coming over!' Grabbing our steel helmets we made a rush for the steps, ran up them past the brazier and the dead Lewis gunner, and so into the trench and onto the firing step, pulling out our revolvers as we went. Sure enough, they were coming at last. The bombardment had stopped and the smoke was clearing. The little field-grey figures could be seen distinctly climbing out of their support line at intervals of perhaps ten yards between each man and hurrying forward down the slight slope across their front line before starting up the long gradual rise to our trench.

Along the whole of our Company frontage, line after line of them sprang up and advanced before being lost to sight in the 'dead ground' at the bottom of the slope. Their trenches must have been jammed with men, for more and more followed. Then the front waves began to advance up the slope, running a few yards and then dropping, keeping in well-extended order and making their rushes in sections, so that the whole line was never moving and exposed at once. But while they so advanced we were not idle. Every man we had, the cook, the two signallers, officers' servants, everybody, lined the parapet and, loading and reloading with desperate energy, poured streams of bullets into each enemy party as it rushed towards us. The rifles crackled and spat, the Lewis guns rose from a high cackle almost to a scream, and the two Vickers guns in the support line, doing their 500 rounds a minute, added a vicious hiss as their bullets passed over our heads. We were getting a bit of our own back after the four and a half hours' bombardment.

When the enemy were first seen to be coming over, the Company Sergeant Major rushed for the spare rifle fitted with a SOS rocket that was kept ready at the top of the dugout steps. It refused to go off when first fired and at the second attempt it only sent up the three coloured (green, red, green) star shells a short distance, but at the third attempt, with a fresh SOS rocket, it sailed up properly and gave a good signal. The reply from the artillery was absolutely nil. Not a single gun responded; apparently the artillery was completely out of action. In ordinary circumstances the sending up of a SOS signal would have brought down a heavy barrage on the enemy front line immediately. This would have been of great assistance to us in helping to repel the attack, but on this most critical occasion not a shell came over. Whether our artillery was temporarily out of action through enemy counter-battery shelling or whether they did not see our signal because of the mist, we never heard.

Immediately after the SOS rockets were fired I joined the men on the nearest fire step and blazed away with the old SOS rifle until it was too hot to hold. But the enemy were steadily advancing and we knew that, if they were once allowed to mass close up to our thin line of wire and rush the trench, we should never be able to hold them. Our only hope was to stop them before they could form up close enough for a charge. By this time we were beginning to have a few casualties from their rifle fire as they covered each other's advances. Standing next to me Sergeant Fuller was wounded in the wrist and was lucky not to be killed, as the bullet hit the magazine of his rifle first and tore the metal across before glancing off onto his wrist. Both the signallers who had left their useless instruments to help in the defence were killed and several others wounded. No. 16 Platoon Lewis gun was working again, though with a large hole torn through the outer barrel. Sydney Lowden's servant was badly wounded in the mouth and nearly choked with blood.

At last we seemed to be holding them. Their rushes grew fewer and less determined. Their casualties were strewn over all the ground on which they had advanced. Every time a man moved he attracted a quick volley of bullets from our line. Then one or two tried to scurry back to their own line and we knew that barring further reinforcements their attack was definitely stopped. Just at this moment, when the position seemed more hopeful, we were startled by the sight of a wounded sergeant of the Lancashire Fusiliers dashing down our trench. The Lancashire Fusiliers of the 52nd Brigade occupied the front line on our immediate right and we soon learned the bad news. Apparently the barrage on their frontage had been more accurate than on ours and they had suffered many casualties from it, so that when the attack came they were unable to withstand it and had ultimately evacuated their front line which was now in the hands of the enemy.

Scarcely a minute later we received ample confirmation of this as a sudden enemy bombing attack down the trench from our right made half a dozen of our men retreat hurriedly to the fire bay where I was standing. I at once collected a few men and rushed up the trench to form a stop or barricade and after a minute's hard work succeeded in pulling down a good deal of the parapet into the trench where our section of the line ended. I left three or four men to hold it and two more men – one of them was my servant Wilkinson – climbed out on the parados of our fire bay to cover them with rifle fire. However, a few minutes later the enemy advanced with bombs again, rushed the step and wounded Wilkinson in the head. They were now in the next fire bay to ours and the situation looked precarious. One German stood on the fire step with head and shoulders above the parapet and threw one of their streamer bombs (with wooden handle) at me as I was standing on the fire step of the next fire bay. It landed on the parapet a few feet short, but as I knew these bombs were not very dangerous I disregarded it, took aim at him with my rifle and fired. I was using a second old rifle at the time, the first having got too hot, and it must have been badly out of sighting for I missed him and before I could reload he disappeared. The bomb exploded but I was not hit.

We held them up for the moment by throwing bombs over into their bay but Sydney Lowden, the senior officer in charge, decided to get the Lewis guns away and evacuate the front line as far as the communication trench. I was left behind with one man, Ramsden's servant Butterfield, as a rear guard to hold the enemy up for as long as possible. The two of us hung on where we were for about five minutes, making as much show as possible with bomb throwing, and then retired steadily down the deserted trench. The risk lay not so much from the enemy bombing party in the trench as from the likelihood of being cut off by the rapid advance of the enemy lying out in No Man's Land when they saw the Lewis guns removed. However, we got safely back and joined the others now manning the communication trench.

Barely a minute after this an extraordinary and unfortunate incident took place. I was still standing near the end of the communication trench close to a new 'stop' which had been built at the corner when Second Lieutenant Dean of B Company rushed up from the rear, snatched a couple of Mills bombs, climbed out of the trench and ran across the open to bomb the enemy in our front line. No bombing party had been formed, no quantity of bombs was available at the moment and no one knew of his intentions or followed to assist him. When he climbed out of the trench in full view of the enemy, Butterfield and I stared after him in amazement. Such brave but really foolhardy action could have but one ending. For the moment he surprised the enemy, threw his two bombs and returned for more, but when he rushed forward again with two of the only remaining half dozen that Butterfield was carrying the enemy were ready for him and before he could throw either of them he was shot through the head and fell dead. The whole thing occupied scarcely a minute. As he started forward for the second time, rash though he was, I felt I could not let him go alone and scrambled up the high side of the trench to follow him, but as I got on the top and before Butterfield could hand me a bomb, the shots rang out and he was killed. I was prepared for almost anything that day, but not for suicide and I at once dropped back into our trench.

Afterwards in April, when we were back at rest, the CO recommended a posthumous VC for Dean and I was asked to write an account of it in support as I was the only officer who clearly saw the action. I made as glowing and laudatory a report as I possibly could for which the CO thanked me, but the application was refused. Later there appeared in both the *History of the 50th Infantry Brigade* and the *West Yorkshire Regiment in the War* the most exaggerated and distorted accounts of this tragic episode: I can only imagine that the authors saw my enthusiastic recommendation and then drew on their imaginations for the rest. What actually happened was as I have stated. Butterfield and I were the only men within ten yards at the time and we saw it all.

After this there was a lull for a time. The enemy did not attempt to advance further and we were busy getting supplies of bombs up the communication trench where we were ('Barnes Avenue') and preparing for a counter-bombing attack to recapture our lost section of front line. The bombing party was principally composed of B Company men and moved forward at about noon. Without much difficulty the whole of our section of the front was cleared again. D Company Sergeant Major was wounded in the hand by a bomb but there were very few other casualties. The Lewis guns were brought forward to their old positions soon afterwards and the line generally reoccupied as before. A good stop was put up across the trench beyond the Company HQ dugout.

For the remainder of the day all was quiet except for a certain amount of artillery shelling on our front line which came from the rear. At first we thought it was from our own guns firing short, but after sending several messages of complaint back to HQ we found that our own artillery was not firing and that these shells came from enemy batteries on our right and left rear. Very rapid advances had been made by the enemy during the morning on our flanks and we were thus left in the most uncomfortable position, being fired at from almost every side at once. I was standing in a fire bay at about 4.00 pm when one of these shells burst on the parados. There were two men in the same bay at the time; one of them was standing on the fire step whilst the other stood in the bottom of the trench by me. A great flash of flame shot across the trench over my shoulder, straight at the feet of the man on the fire step. He fell backwards into the bottom of the trench, as the man by me and I both staggered and rolled over under the concussion of the explosion.

My face was pitted with grit and powder and one or two tiny shell splinters entered near the corner of my left eye, but otherwise I was unhurt. The man by my side was hit in the back and the one on the fire step had his left foot completely burnt off. When I could properly open my eyes and look round I found that the first man had gone, but the other one was lying in the trench looking in a dazed sort of way at the charred grey stump at his ankle where his boot and foot had been a minute before. His leg was apparently numbed for he did not seem to be suffering much pain, so I shouted for stretcher bearers and got him away down the line at once. I was the only officer in the front line at the time as Lowden and Ramsden were having a rest and some food in the support Company HQ. I was feeling a bit dazed and half blinded myself, so I was not sorry when they returned soon afterwards and I was able to go back to the support line to bathe my eye and clear away the bits of metal. It was black and blue for a week afterwards and still shows traces of the slight wound where the specks of metal entered. I was lucky once again!

During the afternoon we got a 'priority' wire from the CO: 'Well done B and D Companies'. Late that night I took a special rum ration round to all the men, but I did not give them more than two-thirds of what had been sent up as I feared that they might become too drowsy after their exhausting day. At about 3.45 am in the morning I was again the only officer on duty in the front line when a long message came up by runner from Captain Clark. It was a detailed instruction to prepare to clear the front line of men, to destroy or bury all we could not carry away and to retire by a given route to 'Maxwell Avenue' which was part of the line of the outer defences of Hermies and Havrincourt. The reason for these orders was that our lines had been driven back for great distances to the north and south of the Cambrai salient and we were in danger of being completely surrounded and cut off. So the great retreat began for us.

THE RETREAT

Immediately upon receipt of these orders I set off along the front line to warn all posts of our impending move. It was a still night with a slight haze close to the ground. The ruined trench with its crumbling parapet and black shadows seemed particularly eerie and cold as my orderly and I slipped along from post to post, answering a low challenge, whispering instructions and passing on again into the darkness. As we approached the last post close to the canal we discovered that my fears about the results of combined fatigue and the rum issue had been realized. A barricade of sandbags had been thrown across the trench and behind it lay two sentries fast asleep. I climbed the barricade and shook them both roughly before they awoke and stared stupidly up at us. It was useless to say much – it had been a trying day for all of us – and I left them to thank their lucky stars that we and not the enemy had arrived.

At about 4.30 am we began to move out leaving Sydney Lowden and twenty men as a rear guard, with orders to fire an occasional burst from their Lewis gun until the last moment to keep up the illusion that the line was still held. We found that Battalion HQ occupied the one miserable dugout in Maxwell Avenue trench and we spent a gloomy, tired day there waiting for something unpleasant to happen. All the news was bad. Our new front line called 'Lurgan Switch' was about a quarter of a mile in front of Maxwell Avenue. The enemy were advancing continuously and came up to it in the early afternoon. Their aeroplanes also appeared to have spotted us in Maxwell Avenue for a number of heavy shells came over within a few feet of the trench and showered us with earth. It was fortunate that none actually hit the trench as it was crowded with men and the casualties would have been heavy.

Away over the canal, amongst the ruins of Havrincourt village, we could see one or two enemy scouts working forward. Later in the day the enemy attacked the East Yorkshires in Lurgan Switch with 'flammenwerfer', but were driven off with the assistance of the men of the 50th Light Trench Mortar Battery who were stationed nearby. Some of the East Yorkshires came running back across the open towards Maxwell Avenue in a panic and I had to get out on top and threaten them with a rifle to drive them back into the trench. This gave away our position completely and soon afterwards an enemy aeroplane flew very low straight along our trench line. I grabbed a Lewis gun and let off a drum at it but without effect. Early the next morning the Colonel ordered me to go forward over the next rise to look out for enemy movement. I could see nothing of importance but they soon spotted me and sent over a few shells, so I hastily dropped into a convenient shell hole for a few minutes. At this time the enemy artillery would fire at the least sign of movement.

During the morning we received orders to retire again as the enemy had captured Velu Wood almost directly in our rear and were also entering Hermies village on our left flank about half a mile away. D Company of the West Yorkshires was to form the rear guard and I was the last man to leave Maxwell Avenue. The order to retire came at about 10.00 am, but we did not get away until 2.00 pm, because the enemy advanced against Lurgan Switch just as our C Company was moving out and they were obliged to man the line again until the attack had been driven off. There was no communication trench running back from Maxwell Avenue, so when at long last the rest of the Battalion had got away we climbed out of the trench and followed them down the slope, across the canal and over the high ground towards Ytres. As we crossed the canal and started up the opposite slope parties of the enemy were seen detrenching from the ruins of Hermies. Some of A Company who remained along the canal bank to the last as a fresh rear guard actually dispersed one party with revolver shots as they advanced rapidly, partly disguised in British uniforms. Enemy field artillery also sent a few rounds over us, but we were in very open not to say scattered formation and I do not know that anyone was hit.

As we pushed on towards Ytres we saw signs of the earlier rapid departure of our artillery. Several dumps of brand-new 3" shells lay beside empty gun emplacements and in one little orchard a 6" howitzer had been left behind even though packed up on its carriage. I suppose there had been no transport available to move it. After a slight detour to avoid enemy machine-gun fire we eventually passed through a new trench line that the 63rd (Royal Naval) Division were hurriedly digging and entered Ytres village. Here we halted for a rest in one of the main streets near the BEF Canteen. The canteen attendants had apparently gone and a large barn nearby, where their very considerable stores were kept, had been left open for all who cared to help themselves. There were large cases and crates of cigarettes etc. piled eight or ten feet high and all the troops in the village had their pockets stuffed with them. There was no point in leaving anything for the enemy, although I suppose the place would be set on fire before the last troops left.

There were men of many regiments and divisions in the village. Our Company had only just fallen in and started on the road towards Bus and Barastre when the enemy began to send over heavy 6" HE. Shell after shell screamed over to crash amongst the houses and along the road beyond us; great clouds of rolling black smoke rose and drifted across the village, while at the same time low-flying enemy aeroplanes raced overhead and poured machine-gun bullets amongst the crowds of men. Orders were at once given to scatter across the fields and our Company melted away in all directions. I did not see them again that day. As I made for a nearby hedge that seemed to be the only form of cover, a man who ran past me was shot through the instep of his right foot by a machine-gun bullet from an aeroplane almost directly overhead. It was only about fifty feet above us and seemed to be able to fire straight down. There is no use in arguing with a machine-gun and little more in trying to bring down an aeroplane with a revolver, so I got out of the way as rapidly as possible. After a few minutes the aeroplanes flew away and I returned to the road.

I soon came across Captain Clark of D Company who was painfully hobbling along in heavy field boots that hurt his sore feet considerably. These lace-up field boots looked very smart and were much fancied by young officers in England and others who had little walking to do, but they were no use to those of us in France who had to march over rough ground for hour after hour, day after day. I had not taken off my Lotus ankle boots for five days, but my feet were still quite comfortable, although they became very sore and swollen after three more days and nights of almost continuous marching as the boot soles became thinner and thinner. By 26 March my bare toe was showing through one boot and the soles were so thin that I could and did feel every stone on the road.

On 23 March Captain Clark limped slowly beside me through the ruins of the village of Bus, but just beyond we came across a discarded bicycle by the roadside so he mounted it and rode comfortably on through the village of Barastre and almost as far as Rocquigny. Here we overtook the tail end of the confused stream of transport of all kinds that jammed the roads for miles back. He was obliged to throw away the bicycle and continue on foot, dodging along amongst the horses and wagons, sometimes on the road but often in the gutter. The road from Barastre to Rocquigny was littered with broken-down transport wagons, dead horses, dumped kit, stores of all kinds and a few dead men here and there. As we passed along, a battery of field artillery came galloping up, swung off the road amongst the coarse grass, swept their guns round, unlimbered their horses and began firing rapidly in the direction of Bertincourt. We left them to it.

At the crossroads at Rocquigny, an MP (military policeman) was directing all men of the 17th Division to an open stretch of ground to the north-west of the village where the battalions and brigades were being reassembled. Here we found most of the officers and men of our Battalion and others continued to wander in during the night. Four of us found a large old grass-covered shell hole – probably made more than a year earlier – in which we made ourselves as comfortable as we could under one large mackintosh sheet and tried to snatch a little sleep. Late that night orders came through that we were to move forward at once, but they were apparently cancelled soon afterwards. We remained in our shell hole until daybreak on the 24th when we got a cold breakfast of sorts and almost immediately moved off by platoons towards Barasatre.

We spread out as a thin outpost line to the south-east of Barastre and the men began to dig themselves in with their entrenching tools on a forward slope of short grass. There was no cover whatever and enemy shelling began shortly. A sergeant lying near me was soon hit in the leg but was taken away on a wheelbarrow. Major Cotton, our Second-in-Command, was hit in the head but was able to walk away to the rear swathed in shell dressings. About this time (perhaps 10.00 am) we heard that the King's Royal Rifle Corps were surrounded in Bus village and several large tanks lumbered forward through our line to their assistance. A lot of shell and machine-gun firing was soon heard near the village and the King's Royal Rifle Corps withdrew successfully.

Soon afterwards we retired to some higher ground about a quarter of a mile farther back and lay alongside a rough cart track that appeared to run from Barastre to Rocquigny. We had been there barely twenty minutes when enemy aeroplanes came over and spotted us. A few minutes later field gun (3") shells began to burst all round. Second Lieutenant Lynch was soon killed and the Adjutant, Captain Neville, was wounded, as well as a number of men. Further orders came up to retire again and we trailed back across the open country by platoons at wide intervals. My platoon and I caught up the party who were carrying Captain Neville; just as we reached them one of the stretcher poles broke and he was thrown to the ground. Luckily I noticed a party of stretcher bearers from a Scottish regiment of another division about a quarter of a mile away and they agreed to take him on their stretcher. The next time I saw him was in Whitley Bay.

As we approached the main Bapaume–Peronne road the whole countryside presented a strange and wild appearance. Small parties of troops of many regiments were moving in various directions. The road itself was simply choked with transport, so tanks and batteries of artillery were hurrying across country. To the north and east dense clouds of black smoke were drifting across the sky from burning stores that could not be removed. To the south near Le Transloy great sheets of flame shot up from a long line of huts steeped in petrol. Colonel Simner, now without either Second-in-Command or Adjutant, hurried from one platoon to another to give us the latest orders which were for all parties to make their way independently via Ligny-Thilloy and Le Sars to Courcelette where the Division would reassemble.

The Bapaume–Peronne road is similar to other 'routes nationale' with a partly 'pavé' surface and a line of tall trees along each side. Our route lay straight across it and as I stood by the far side watching my men dodge through the stream of traffic, I suddenly noticed someone galloping furiously towards us along the extreme edge of the road. He proved to be a staff officer with fresh orders. We were only to retire as far as Gueudecourt and take up a new defensive line there. Unfortunately our A and B Companies had already pushed on before us and never received these orders; we did not see them again for several days, so C and D Companies and Headquarters Staff were left to represent the Battalion in the line. As it was, A and B Companies retired to Courcelette and ultimately to Havrincourt 4 miles west of Albert where they were formed into a temporary 'brigade' together with several hundreds of stragglers from other divisions and commenced reorganization.

In the meantime we trudged on towards Gueudecourt, falling out by the side of the road just short of the village to rest. Here we remained until dusk, not knowing what was going on and most of us too tired to care very much. We learnt later that we were surrounded by the enemy on three sides and that Corps Headquarters had given up our part of the Brigade as lost. Colonel Simner and Captain Brown, the Intelligence Officer, had left us to try to find the Brigadier and obtain fresh orders. Just after dusk we fell in again along the road under the leadership of Captain Peters of A Company, who was now acting as Adjutant. The head of the column comprised the two remaining Companies, C and D, and was amongst the first to enter the broken-down houses of the village (Gueudecourt). After a few minutes wait, a message came down the line for me to go to the front. I found Captain Peters studying a map with the aid of a flash lamp and as I had some reputation for map reading he had sent for me to help him find the only possible route out of the enemy circle that was fast closing in on us.

We had scarcely begun to consider the position when two dark figures were seen quietly approaching from amongst the ruins. They were promptly halted and challenged. A stage whisper replied 'Brigadier, 50th Brigade' and a moment later Brigadier General Yatman and Lieutenant Wilson, his ADC, came forward covered by our revolvers. The situation was really pretty desperate: we knew that large numbers of the enemy were closing in on three sides, but we were not sure how close they were to our flanks or whether they had already joined hands behind us and so cut off our retreat completely. The only thing to do was to make the attempt to escape before dawn – after that it would be hopeless.

All men were ordered to fix bayonets and all officers to hold their revolvers in their hands. Then, in complete silence and led by the Brigadier, we commenced our march through the night. At night all marching seems tiring and all distances great. This one seemed never-ending as we slogged along without a word or a smoke, of course, peering right and left into the darkness and half expecting a sudden volley of rifle fire at every turn in the road. Which way we went and how long we marched I do not know, but by about midnight we had safely escaped to a point between Eaucourt l'Abbé (Warlencourt-Eaucourt) and Le Sars, and lay down by the roadside to rest. Here we got in touch with the 2nd Division and after a freezing cold wait of a couple of hours we moved forward again to a slope of rough ground at Destremont

Farm, nearly half a mile east of Eaucourt l'Abbé, and took up a line amongst the old grass-covered shell holes on the right flank of the 2nd Division. At this time C and D Companies mustered about 150 men altogether; D Company was scattered in little groups in shell holes as a 'front line', with C Company similarly disposed in close support. Our one and only surviving Lewis gun, and that with a damaged outer casing and little ammunition, was presided over by Second Lieutenant Ramsden ('Babs') on our left flank.

It was about 3.00 am on the 25th when we became settled in this position. After taking my turn at patrolling the 'line' I slept on the wet grass for a couple of hours and awoke stiff, cold and very hungry. On the previous day a young fellow of about nineteen, whose name I forget, had attached himself to me and offered to become my servant in place of Wilkinson who was wounded on the 21st. At about 6 o'clock on this morning he appeared with a sandbag from which he produced half a loaf of very dry bread and several pieces of sticky and dusty bacon. We were not particular in those days and I was delighted to see him. It was not long before he got a small fire going and we were ravenously eating fried bacon and bread soaked in fat. Our last meal had been 'tea' at 4 o'clock on the previous day and this breakfast proved to be the only meal of the day for me, with the exception of a few very small 'thumbnail' biscuits and some cheese and an onion, so it was a very good thing he turned up with this bread and bacon when he did.

As I have said, on our left were troops of the 2nd Division and on our right I believe were some of the East Yorkshires and Dorsets of our own Brigade. Our job was to hold up the enemy along this improvised 'line' for as long as possible. It seemed to me that the position was perfectly hopeless and unsound from the start, and so it proved to be. We were halfway down the reverse slope of a ridge – that is to say we faced up the hillside – and behind us the ground fell away in a medium slope for perhaps 200 yards. After that it rose again for about 500 yards to the top of the next ridge where a cluster of tree stumps and fallen masonry marked the one-time village of Eaucourt l'Abbé. We had no line trenches or communication trenches and could not stir a foot from our shell holes except in the open; we had no more food and no reserve of ammunition; we had no supporting troops behind us and no artillery at all; and we had not even seen one of our own aeroplanes for days. On our left flank a rough road ran down the slope to the rear and in the grass bank on the far side of it was one dugout now used as Battalion HQ, including Colonel Simner (who had now rejoined us) and Captain Peters. No one could reach this dugout except across the open road.

At about 8.00 am enemy advanced scouts began to creep over the top of the ridge in front of us and were immediately lost to view amongst the shell holes, heather and thick grass that covered the ridge. We fired at any we could see, but I do not think we caused many casualties, for looking up the slope against the brightness of the sky seemed to make the hillside darker and objects on it more difficult to distinguish. After a while they brought two or three machine-guns into action, though I could not spot where they were, and bullets began to whistle through the grass in the most unpleasant fashion. I had no rifle and a revolver was useless at that range so I lay full length in the grass behind a strip of rusty iron that was partly embedded in the ground. I do not know if it was an old sniping plate left there since 1916 or part of a field gun shield or even an agricultural implement of some sort, but I was very glad it was there as bullets rattled against it many times.

Ramsden was putting up a great fight with his Lewis gun and also with a few rifle grenades he had found somewhere, but his ammunition was running out and the position was fast becoming critical. A man in a shell hole near me cried out that he was hit and I made a dive to him. He had a bullet through his stomach that had come out at the back and there was little I could do for him. He seemed numbed and not in any pain. I told him to keep warm and I would try to get him away, though I knew that there were no stretcher bearers and no ambulances, and very little chance of escape for any of us.

Soon after 10.00 am a runner got through from the right to say that the line had broken and the men were in full retreat – our right flank was 'in the air'. Still we hung on, though the barrage became heavier. At 10.30 am we saw on the high ground on our left a man of the 2nd Division in a long trench coat spring up and race off towards the rear. A minute later their whole line broke and scores of little figures in the distance were running and stumbling in a wild stampede for safety. Then the machine-gun barrage that swept over us seemed to double in intensity, so that we could scarcely hear each other shout above the drumming and chatter of the guns and the scream of the bullets. After two or three minutes of this deluge of fire, to which we could by now make practically no reply, scores of the enemy sprang to their feet and came leaping down the hill towards us, some shooting as they came, some shouting 'Kamerad' as if they knew we could do nothing but surrender. That was the end.

I saw no man hold up his hands in surrender but everyone turned and ran, hoping against hope that somehow he might elude the bullets and gain the crest of the ridge behind in safety. It was the only thing to try for; to remain meant certain capture or death; but that breathless rush for perhaps 500 yards up an open slope with the expectation of a bullet in the back every moment was one of the most unpleasant experiences I ever had. That so many of us did get through was due to the fact that the enemy barrage slackened and lifted as they advanced, but even so the bullets whistled past me and tossed up tiny sprays of earth on every side. One man rushed up to me clutching his hand. 'My hand, what shall I do, they've hit my hand,' he cried. I pointed to the top

of the ridge: 'Run, you fool,' I said. As I started up the slope
I looked back for Ramsden and saw him running down the
road trailing the battered Lewis gun behind him. I had
thrown away my heavy pack at the beginning and halfway
up the slope my bulky haversack swung and knocked against
my legs. I thought to myself, 'Perhaps it's my life or this', and
let it go. I have often wondered since if I might have saved it
after all. Very probably I might – possibly I might not.

At the top of the ridge I found myself close to Lieutenant
Brown, Lieutenant Lowden and a number of the men. We all
streamed down the opposite slope and up a steep little rise
beyond. An officer of another regiment, badly wounded in
the head, was being held up by a couple of men and I gave a
hand in half carrying him down the slope until he was taken
over by some friends of his own, but he died before they got
much farther. There was an old trench along the top of the
next rise where in an attempt to form another line we
collected about thirty men who had succeeded in escaping,
but their nerve was gone and we could not hold them. In a
few minutes the enemy reached the Eaucourt l'Abbé ridge
and opened fire. When one man was hit in the stomach and
rolled out of the trench, the rest broke and ran and were
soon lost to sight. Second Lieutenant E. Smith, who had
joined the Battalion from an officers' school on the night of
the 23rd, was close to me at the time and when everyone else
seemed to have gone we followed.

In this action at Destrement Farm we lost Captain 'Doc'
Hunter (the MO) and Captain Peters killed, Lieutenant
Hartnell and Lieutenant Lowden wounded, and Colonel
Simner and Lieutenant Shurrock taken prisoner: six officer
casualties in three hours out of a total of ten present. 'Doc'
Hunter DSO was supposed to be on the German 'Black List'
for having led an attack at some time though a non-
combatant officer. His RAMC corporal was most devoted to
him and tried to get him away in a barrow when he was very
severely wounded at Destrement Farm, but the 'Doc' told

him to leave him and took a large overdose of morphine as he was determined never to fall into the hands of the enemy alive.

Second Lieutenant Smith and I could see three separate columns of retiring troops in the distance, but we could not overtake them so we went on alone across the Albert–Baupaume Road and over the rough ground in the direction of Miraumont. After about 3 miles we came to a road and noticed a couple of men on it half a mile ahead. At first we thought of following them but at that moment a large shell passed overhead and burst on the road beyond, so we promptly turned into the rough again and kept at a respectful distance from it. At this time the enemy shelled the main roads and crossings continuously. It was now after one o'clock and we were very hungry. Smith had a few small round biscuits and we sat in a hollow and ate them. After a short rest we set out again and on approaching the road once more we found the two men we had seen a little while before. Both were dead. One lay huddled in the rough grass, the other with arms outstretched in the centre of the road but with his head lying in the gutter.

Another quarter of an hour's walking brought us close to Miraumont railway station, but on the edge of a high cliff that fell away almost sheer down to the lines. We spent ten minutes finding a way down and then ran across the half dozen or more lines and went up the approach slope where we had seen some mounted officers in the distance. These proved to be a Divisional General and his staff and when I asked him if he knew where the 17th Division was situated he replied that he did not even know where his own Division was, but that he was going to make for Puisieux-au-Mont and advised us to do the same. They then galloped off and left us to decide what to do. By this time we had added one man of the West Yorkshire Regiment and two Lancashire Fusiliers to our party, so the five of us continued up the slope but well away from the town and station where huge shells were now beginning to fall. On the grass in an orchard we found half a large cheese which someone had evidently abandoned hastily, so we sat down and made a light meal of cheese and the few biscuits we had left. We then struck out in the direction of Puisieux-au-Mont or where we thought it would be, but after getting onto the high ground and seeing the miles of waste land rolling away in the distance, we decided to turn to the left towards Albert in the hope of coming across some other parties.

My boot soles were getting thin and my feet very sore so it was something of a relief when we got down into the valley and onto the smooth-surfaced road that ran from Miraumont to Beaucourt-sur-l'Anere and on to Albert. We joined the road close to Beaucourt and found several parties of men of different divisions, but none of ours. It was getting dusk and cold as we reached Beaucourt railway station and we were very tired and fed up, so we entered a shed on the platform, partly to rest and partly to see if there was anything inside that would be of any use to us. We found two or three old blankets and a box on the floor containing a few onions. These proved to be my supper for that night and my topcoat by day and bedclothes by night for several days to come. As we sat eating our onions we saw a ragged column of tired and gloomy looking men come over the railway bridge and discovered that they were a mixed party of troops of the 17th Division. We joined them at once and climbed the steep hillside to the north-west of the railway where we spent a cold and miserable night in an old chalk trench.

It began to drizzle with rain in the early morning and soon after daybreak, without any breakfast, all the officers and men of 50 Brigade were formed into a column and began one more march in retreat. Colonel James of the Lancashire Fusiliers (Labour Battalion) was the senior officer and in command. After a weary march of seven or eight miles we reached Forceville where we were delighted to find a half limber of provisions and a bottle of rum. Nearly all the French civilians had fled. We left at about 9 o'clock and arrived at Hénencourt soon after midday where we found A and B Companies of our Battalion under the temporary command of Major Hall. They all looked very spick and span after their days of rest and reorganization, but I am afraid none of my pre-war friends would have recognized me. My clothes were torn and covered with dust, my face was dirty and lined with sweat and I had not had a shave for days; my left eye was coloured various shades as the result of the shell on the 21st, my big toe was showing through a hole in my left boot and in place of a trench coat I was carrying my filthy dark-brown blanket.

I went to report to Major Hall and after one good look at me he told me to go away at once, have my eye attended to and then have a few days' rest with the transport. I learnt that our transport was lying at Forceville so after a wash I started on my travels once more. This time I was accompanied by Second Lieutenant Darnborough who had been with our Battalion only a few days and was leaving to join the Machine-Gun Corps. We got a good meal in a French estaminet at Warloy-Baillon and then trudged on to Forceville, which we reached long after dark. The moon was almost full and threw long shadows of silent, deserted houses across the village street. Our boots seemed to make an enormous clatter on the rough road as we went from end to end in search of the transport. When we did find them they seemed anything but pleased to see us and were evidently suffering from chronic 'wind up'. This is generally the case with men on the outer fringe of danger; it is not so commonplace and continuous as to make them heedless of it, but it lurks in the background as a horrible possibility that may become a fact at any time; sometimes it so preys upon their nerves that they are useless when their fears come true.

We found Lieutenant Quartermaster Haywood and Lieutenant Gill, the Transport Officer, pouring over some ration sheets by the light of one flickering candle. They said Boche planes were out on these moonlight nights and they sheltered their candle as if it had been The Needles lighthouse. After my experiences in the line the idea of being scared of two or three bombing aeroplanes seemed ridiculous and childish. When they told us that they had no accommodation for us with the transport and knew of nowhere else, we promptly said goodnight and left them. We wandered back through the village (Forceville) wondering whether to break into one of the empty houses, when at the main crossroads we noticed through a gateway in a high wall that a light was shining in the house beyond.

After some hard knocking the door was opened a few inches by a very old and frightened Frenchman. However, he allowed us to enter when I explained to him in my sketchy French that we only wanted shelter for the night. He led us into a large but poorly furnished room where his wife, an old woman of about seventy-odd, was sitting by a small wood fire. These two poor old people had been left behind when the village was deserted, probably because they had nowhere else to go, and lived on alone in this gloomy old house, trembling at every sound they heard. I cheered them up as well as I could in my bad French by assuring them that the enemy were definitely stopped by now and would never get as far as Forceville, but my efforts were suddenly and most unfortunately discounted by the violent explosion of a shell in their own orchard just beyond the house, which rattled all their windows and sent the poor old woman almost into hysteria. It was a chance shot and no more followed but she continued to wring her hands and wail: 'Oh, this terrible war, this horrible war.' She calmed down after a while and they took the lamp and a family Bible and went off to bed, leaving us to a good night's sleep on the carpet by the fire.

In the morning after breakfast on 27 March, we left them with many thanks and returned to where the transport had been, only to find that they had departed during the night and there was no one to say where they had gone. Two days before he was killed Doc Hunter had examined my eye and advised me to have it attended to if ever I got back to civilization, so I decided to bother no more about the transport but to make for the big General Hospital at Doullens. Darnborough and I parted on the Forceville road: he went on to Acheux to join his unit and I turned off for Léalvillers en route to Doullens. On the way I was pleased to see a battalion of New Zealanders going up to the front – some fresh troops at last. Beyond Léalvillers I came across a battery of field artillery and bought a feed of bacon and eggs from their mess. After trudging on a few more miles I had a lift on a lorry to a village near Doullens where I spent the night.

The next morning (28th) I walked into Doullens over the old bridge and in the main street I asked a passing private soldier if he could direct me to a barber's shop. He told me that he was the servant of the Town Major and that if I cared to go with him to his lodgings he would lend me a safety razor and I could have a good clean up. I expect I looked a bit of a wreck with my two days beard, my rough Tommy's tunic (all officers went into the line wearing private's tunics) and with my old blanket still carried over my arm. I felt better after this and after a good lunch at an hotel in the middle of the town I made my way towards the castle which was then doing duty as a general hospital.

The castle was a huge old place on a small hill closely overlooking the town. When I got to the top of the very long drive leading up to the main entrance I found myself amongst a large cluster of waiting ambulances, some discharging wounded for registration and treatment in the hospital and some picking up ticketed and labelled men for transfer to the railway station and probably England. I went in to an immense hall that was simply crowded with people, though there was no hurry or confusion and very little noise. Wounded men were all over, some lying on the floor on stretchers, some sitting on benches, many standing; all waiting patiently either for attention or for removal as the convoys were made up. Six or seven doctors were in different parts of the hall examining wounds, cleaning, washing and bandaging, assisted by a number of women nurses.

As I stared round the hall I noticed a platform at the far end on which an operating table stood. A man was lying on it and an operation was being performed. As I watched the surgeon finished sawing through the patient's right leg close to the thigh and the attendant nurse picked it up and placed it in a long basket under the table. I went forward to a large desk where an RAMC corporal was taking down the particulars of all casualties as they arrived and afterwards I passed on to be examined by one of the doctors. He said that my eye wound looked healthy and he gave me an injection against tetanus, though he said I should have had it days before. There was nothing more to be done and I went out again into the open air. More ambulances were arriving almost every minute bringing grimy, weary men with torn clothes and bloody bandages, men of all ranks and all regiments, some grim and silent as they limped into the hall, some moaning in delirium as they were swiftly carried in on often dripping stretchers. These are the realities, the very commonplaces of war, when the brilliant uniforms are discarded and the brass bands left at home.

As I passed the ambulances I saw an RAMC man come out of a building on my left and I asked him if he could get me a pair of clean socks. He said that he would and that if I cared to I could have a hot bath as well, as this building contained the doctors' bathrooms which were not being used just then. I went in with him at once and gladly allowed him to cut and peel off the remains of my old long-suffering socks which had so pressed into and mingled with my skin that I did not recognize my feet at all when I saw them once again, the first time for ten days or more. My toes were pressed into each other and stuck together, and my feet were all covered with little creases and wrinkles as fingers may become when kept for long in hot water. After my bath and change I strolled down towards the town again, meeting on the way a stream of local townspeople hurrying towards the castle and all carrying quantities of bedding with them. I learnt that every night the enemy planes came over to bomb Doullens and had so scared the French civilians that they removed at dusk to the huge caves that ran under the castle hill. I went back to my hotel for dinner and afterwards, upon enquiry of the proprietor, was offered a bedroom upstairs for only three francs if I cared to take it – as for himself he was sleeping in the cellar! I was not worried by the thought of bombs and slept soundly right through the night so I do not know if the planes came over or not on that occasion.

In the morning of 29 March I went to see about getting some sort of coat to take the place of my dirty old blanket. Burberrys had a branch shop in Doullens so I obtained the assistance of an interpreter from the French Military Mission and bought a mackintosh for about 70 francs. From there I went to the railway station to ask the RTO (Railway Transport Officer) the present position of the 17th Division. He could not give me any definite information but after lunch I turned my back on Doullens and after some 'lorry jumping' came across the West Yorkshire transport outside Puchevillers. They were on the point of moving forward to Warloy-Baillon so I went with them on one of the GS wagons and reached the new quarters at dusk. My big valise containing my sleeping bag and various spare kit had been travelling round the countryside on the transport ever since the retreat began, so I took it off the GS wagon and made my bed in a large kind of attic in the house where we were billeted. Partly as a result of the anti-tetanus injection I was feeling very tired and washed out, and I spent the next two days mostly sleeping and dozing in my sleeping bag. On the afternoon of the 31st I went up to Hénencourt to arrange billets for the Battalion which was coming out of the line that night.

April

On 3 April we all marched back on rest to Pernois. After three days there we moved on to Bonneville where we spent a week refitting and reorganizing. Amongst other things Battalion Headquarters had to be reformed. We had a new CO, Lieutenant Colonel Thomas, a new Second-in-Command, Major Waite, a new Adjutant, Captain Williams, and I was made Intelligence Officer once again. I was thus the only old officer of the Battalion now in the Headquarters.

While at Bonneville I had to act twice as prosecutor in courts martial. On the first occasion I had something of a battle of wits with Captain Penty who was taking his usual role on such occasions as 'prisoner's friend'. This position really amounts to counsel for the defence. The prisoner was D Company cook who was accused of striking D Company Quartermaster Sergeant. Striking a superior officer is a serious crime in the Army. Captain Penty was a wily sort of fellow who had been with the Battalion for a long time and was well used to acting as 'prisoner's friend'. On the night before the trial he spent three hours or more with the prisoner during which he prepared a speech for the defence running into about a dozen sheets of foolscap. The charge was simply 'striking a superior officer', but Penty's defence was on the lines that the prisoner had taken his rum ration that night out of an old and dirty tin which had so intoxicated him that he was not responsible for his actions; and also that owing to his earlier years of life at sea during which he had sustained some injury to his head, he was peculiarly susceptible to rum and was very easily affected.

Penty even went so far as to drag in the man's mother who he said had died in an asylum. After marshalling this collection of extenuating circumstances and sob stuff, Penty was so pleased with himself and so confident of his defence that he bragged openly before me and other officers of the certainty of the discharge of the prisoner and the complete and indeed overwhelming discomfiture of the prosecution. All these details came out during the actual trial but Penty, in his self-confidence and also no doubt in an attempt to frighten me into thinking my first case a hopeless one, had indicated the line he intended to take and I sat down to think out some way of getting round it.

An hour before the court martial assembled I went among the witnesses for the prosecution finding out exactly what evidence they could give and arranging my case. By the time proceedings began I was feeling much more satisfied. When the preliminaries were over I was called upon by the President of the Court to state the case for the prosecution and after a brief speech I called my first witness, a sergeant. In reply to my questions he swore that he saw the prisoner enter the Quartermaster's Stores shortly before the 'crime' was committed and that the prisoner was not drunk but perfectly sober. I looked at Penty's face – it was, as the saying goes, a study! I then called my second witness who also swore that he saw the prisoner at the time and that he was not drunk. I looked at Penty again and his face was still a 'study' – a study in red this time. Shortly afterwards when he was called to make the case for the defence, he got up, shuffled all his papers, glared at me and growled out that the prosecution had presented the case in what he considered to be an unfair and most unexpected way, and that he must ask for an adjournment of the Court so that he could rearrange his defence! When the Court reassembled in the afternoon Penty's defence was still quite out of joint and the prisoner was ultimately sentenced to two years' imprisonment. Penty would not look at me for days afterwards.

During our stay at Bonneville I acquired a new servant and a good one he proved to be. Butterworth was a short stocky little fellow with rosy cheeks and a jerky manner, but he was an excellent and conscientious worker, and both loyal and reliable. I never knew what happened to the young servant I had at Destremont Farm on 25 March, though I heard a rumour that he had been killed. Butterworth remained with me until 12 August when he was wounded in the hand and returned to England. Before the war he had been a hawker and lived at Crookes in Sheffield.

On 12 April we moved to Raincheval and on the 14th our Division relieved the 63rd (Royal Naval) Division in the sector between Mesnil and Beaumont Hamel. The East Yorkshires and Dorsets held the front line at first and we were in reserve round the village of Englebelmer. Some of the houses in Englebelmer were not much damaged and for two or three nights I stayed in a house that must have belonged to a watchmaker or collector for it was crowded with watches and clocks of all sorts and sizes. On the second day I took a few of my observers up to make a new Observation Post on the top of a low ridge between Englebelmer and Mesnil. In order to fix the position I took a compass bearing on the hanging statue of the Madonna and Child on the tower of Albert Church which could be seen in the far distance. We heard that our heavy artillery was shelling the tower because enemy machine-guns were firing from it and when we went to our new OP the next day the statue had gone.

On about 19th April we relieved the East Yorkshires in the front line. Battalion HQ was in the cellar of a red-brick house in Mesnil. The front line was a roughly made and very irregular trench on the eastern slope of the valley of the River Ancre and faced straight across the valley to the heights of Thiepval Ridge opposite. On the 21st the enemy attacked this line and captured several advance posts held by the 10th Notts and Derbys on our right and also one forward post of ours that was situated at the bottom of the slope close to the river. Later in the day orders were received to counter-attack the following morning and recapture the lost positions. I was ordered by the CO to occupy an old OP amongst some trees at the top of the ridge and to watch and report on the progress of the attack.

I reached my post at 5.30 am and the attack began at 6.00 am, but the smoke from the enemy counter barrage of trench mortars was so thick that I could see nothing at all, so at about 6.30 am I sent my men back to Battalion HQ and went down the open slope to the front line myself to find out what was happening. The counter-attack was not a success. Second Lieutenants King and Daysh had been killed and the position on the right flank was still very obscure. The circumstances surrounding Daysh's death were particularly sad. A few days previously he had received a very urgent message to say that his wife was dangerously ill and he had applied for special leave to be allowed to go and see her. The sanction for this leave was received at Battalion HQ about an hour after he was killed.

On the right there was a gap in the line for about a quarter of a mile where the 'trench' merely consisted of a series of occasional holes in the ground, but in the trenches beyond I could see a party of perhaps fifty men apparently moving in our direction. The crew of a nearby Vickers machine-gun assured me that these were enemy troops though they appeared to me to be our own, so I began to work my way across the gap towards them while the machine-gunners volunteered to keep me covered with their gun. By the time I had got about a third of the way, one of the supposed enemy had also advanced in my direction to within almost fifty yards. When I shouted 'Who are you?' he replied 'OC front line.' He was Second Lieutenant Knight of D Company, an eccentric individual of peculiar appearance who remained with the Battalion for about two months, during which time he was chiefly occupied in forming a concert party and singing comic songs.

Later the same day we were relieved by the 52nd Brigade and went into reserve at Forceville. It was my job to lead the Headquarters staff back from Mesnil to Forceville and as we plodded over the rough grass on the high ground we had a rather unusual experience. We were far from a road (roads were very often shelled at night) when I noticed a lighted red lamp standing on the grass a short distance ahead. At first I was puzzled to account for this, but was not left in doubt for long as with a great flash and a roar a shell went screaming over our heads towards the German lines. We had stumbled across the line of fire of one of our own heavy batteries. We changed direction at once and reached Forceville safely half an hour later.

On 24 April Lieutenant Colonel G.K. Butt joined the Battalion as its new CO and acting Lieutenant Colonel W.E. Thomas left us. Colonel Thomas was a brave, fair-minded man and a gentleman; Colonel Butt was neither – it was an exceedingly poor exchange. Two days later, on the 26th, we returned to the front line, but on the right Battalion sector this time, so that part of our front was in Aveluy Wood. On the first night the new CO made a tour of the front line and I accompanied him. As Intelligence Officer I generally accompanied whoever was CO in his tours around the line, but this occasion was more amusing and interesting than others. It was about 1.00 am on the 27th when we started and, led by a guide, we promptly plunged into the thickest part of the wood which is about one mile deep and about one and a half miles long, intersected with numerous straight 'rides' running at right angles to each other.

We soon came across a gun pit of a Light Trench Mortar Battery and were just in time to be almost deafened by the firing of two or three of their Stokes Mortars. Here the CO bumped his head severely against a fallen tree. He was already getting irritable and 'windy', but after a few minutes we went on again, crashing through the undergrowth until we reached one of the open 'rides' down which we crept as silently as possible towards the front line. The 'line' consisted of about six small and quite isolated posts situated in the thick undergrowth of the wood with great trees towering above. When we reached the first post our guide left us as he knew the route no farther and from there onwards at each post we picked up a fresh guide who conducted us to the next. Tree roots and brambles straggled over the ground and the CO tripped over most of them, swearing in a whisper to himself each time as he scrambled to his feet. The enemy posts were somewhere lower down in the wood, but we heard and saw nothing of them and got back to the Battalion HQ dugout at about 3.00 am, after which I got about three hours' sleep before beginning another busy day. During these tours in the line I never got more than four hours' sleep out of the twenty-four and not always that.

May

After a few days in reserve we returned to the front line but on the left Battalion sector this time, with our HQ in the red-brick house close to the Mesnil church. We used to enter this house very respectably by the front door and proceed along the hall to the cellar steps which were close to the back door, but we had to be careful and quick in turning down these steps, especially at night, as an enemy machine-gun firing up the line and over the ridge spattered bullets in the broken-down back doorway at fairly frequent intervals. Our cookhouse was a kind of small cellar very close to the church, only thirty yards from the house. During some indiscriminate enemy shelling one morning a chance shell hit the remains of the old clock tower and brought it down with a considerable crash and clouds of dust and mortar almost on top of our expected lunch. When one or two of us hurried out to see what was wrong we found the cookhouse entrance almost completely blocked with fallen masonry and rubbish, with both the cooks and our lunch in a very grubby and unhappy condition. Fortunately nobody was hurt – but the lunch was.

On 8 May we were relieved by a Battalion of the 63rd (Royal Naval) Division and marched back to rest at Arquèves. Here we remained for a fortnight, training and reorganizing, and I had a fairly busy time in the Orderly Room, though I did manage to get out for a few rides on the Doctor's sedate charger. While we were at Arquèves two events took place which were of special interest to me at the time. The first and unpleasant event was the departure of Captain Williams, the Adjutant, and the arrival in his place of Captain Anderson, an earlier Adjutant of the Battalion, who had been away on extended leave. Captain Anderson was an objectionable person in many ways; he was cowardly, blustering and sly, and I soon had several rows with him.

The second and much more pleasant event was a Battalion Dinner arranged by Major (afterwards Lieutenant Colonel) Gibson, DSO, MC. This was a great and indeed boisterous success and will no doubt long remain in the memories of those who were fortunate enough to be present. The Brigadier and Brigade staff were present and whisky, sherry and port were very much in evidence from the beginning and the effects of them even more in evidence towards the close. The dinner was held in a very large barn at the back of one of the farms in the village and long trestle tables were set down the centre, while a platform at one side was occupied by our regimental orchestra. Several speeches were made, many toasts were drunk and 'The Muffin Man' was sung with great enthusiasm. 'The Muffin Man' was a round song that had been adopted by the 17th Division long before and was always sung on these occasions. At half past ten the orchestra left and at about the same time Knight, who was sitting near me, disappeared under the table pulling the cloth and a bottle of port after him. Proceedings then began to get hilarious and only came to an end at about 1.00 am when Captain Abrahams (our new Doctor), after singing a song on the platform, took a flying leap onto the middle table and brought it down with a great clatter. Major Gibson and several others got the CO to bed; I more or less carried Abrahams to our tent where he slept with me; and Haywood, the Lieutenant Quartermaster, after falling into the farm sewage pond, spent the remainder of the night on some straw in a barn.

On 26 May the Battalion moved up to Acheux en route for the front line, but that same afternoon a message arrived from Division for an officer and a number of men who needed a rest to be sent down to the 'Divisional Wing' at Talmas and I was chosen to go. Ramsden and I were probably the only officers who had been through the whole of the fighting in the Retreat in March and were still with the Battalion; he joined our party at Talmas the day after I did. Officers and men from all the battalions of the Division were there and those of our Brigade were billeted in a large house and adjacent outbuildings. There were about nine officers who slept in the house upstairs with a mess and kitchens downstairs.

June

We remained at Talmas until 25 June enjoying splendid weather and having a good time generally. There were about 150 NCOs and men in our miniature Brigade and we took them out each morning for marches and simple manoeuvres. We returned for lunch at 1.00 pm, after which they had the remainder of the day free. One day Captain 'Billy' Burne turned up at Talmas en route for the Battalion after a spell in hospital. He was as wild as ever and got very drunk that night, but at about 11 o'clock I got him back to his billet in an estaminet, pushed him upstairs and left him lying under a billiard table to sleep it off. He was a big, dark, powerful fellow, good natured and generous to others, but an utter fool to himself. While I was on Divisional Wing I was always in command of the West Yorkshire section and several times in command of the whole 'brigade' when the senior officer, Captain Billy Williams of the East Yorkshires, had not quite got over 'the night before'.

I always disliked Captain Anderson, the Battalion Adjutant, and had had several disputes with him as I have mentioned before. About a week after I reached Talmas I received a note from him to say that the CO (Colonel Butt) had decided to appoint a fresh Intelligence Officer and that I must return to my Company when I rejoined the Battalion. It appeared that a certain circular to the Battalion requiring the CO's report had been received two days before I left for Talmas. It had been found amongst my papers, still unattended to, about five days after I had left and Brigade had complained of the delay. Of course I knew about this circular and in my reply to the Adjutant I pointed out that I had twice taken it to the CO for his attention, but each time he had refused to look at anything except what was very urgent, which this was not. Consequently it was not my fault if this circular had been left unanswered in my special folder marked 'Immediate Attention' for five days after I had left. I did not hear any more from the Adjutant, but I was not at all sorry on that account because I had been fed up with the present Battalion HQ for some time and was not the least disappointed at the idea of returning to D Company once more. Colonel Butt and Captain Anderson in one Headquarters were a combination sufficient to sicken anybody.

By 25 June the Battalion had come out on rest and were billeted a few miles from Talmas at Rubempré, where Ramsden and I joined them and were attached to D Company, although Ramsden was really the Lewis Gun Officer. We spent an enjoyable fortnight here: ordinary training and parades were interspersed with horse shows, boxing competitions and so on. Ramsden and I were billeted in the upstairs billiard room of an estaminet in the main street. Ramsden's bed was close under one of the back windows and one night enemy aeroplanes came over and dropped a large bomb in the orchard at the back, smashing Ramsden's window in innumerable splinters all over his bed. Fortunately his face was not cut and an hour afterwards we were both fast asleep again. We went to look at the hole next day and found it was four feet deep and about ten feet across.

July

Four or five days before the end of our fortnight the Battalion was put on half an hour's notice to move, with the result that everyone had to sleep partly dressed so that they could turn out almost at once on the alarm being given. It eventually sounded at about 1.00 am on the morning of 10 July and we marched steadily forward until breakfast time, then rested during the middle of the day and relieved the 12th Division in reserve trenches near Senlis in the evening. We remained in these trenches sending forward nightly working parties until 16 July when we took over a forward sector in front of Bouzincourt. The West Yorkshires were in the support lines at first and we occupied some half-finished chalky trenches about half a mile in front of Bouzincourt village. The weather was very wet, the trenches were undrained and without revetments or dugouts, and we spent a rather miserable six days in this locality.

Raids into the enemy's trenches and posts had been carried out frequently at varying places along the British front ever since the opposing forces had firmly dug themselves in and 'open warfare' had been given up. The raiding parties had varied in numbers from two or three to a thousand or more, and the duration of the raids from a few minutes to perhaps an hour. The main purpose had been to identify the particular enemy troops occupying the area raided, as well as to do as much damage as possible. The importance of identification was rated very highly, for it was largely by means of the identification provided by these raids that the disposition of the enemy front-line troops and reserves could be ascertained.

It was on about 23 July that we learned that our Company had been detailed to make a raid in a week's time. We were at once withdrawn to a reserve position behind Bouzincourt in order to train and prepare for the great event. The strength of the raiding party was to be four officers and seventy men; the objective was a sunken road on the top of the ridge overlooking Albert. This sunken road was situated some little distance behind the enemy front- and support-line trenches and about 300 yards from our own front line. Captain M.F. Smith was to be in command in the centre and I was to lead No. 1 Party on the right, with Second Lieutenant Appleyard in support with No. 3 Party which was also under my orders, while Second Lieutenant Kirk, with a support party under a sergeant, was to lead No. 2 Party on the left. The actual advance was practised several times on ground marked out with white tape and the men also studied a clay model and aeroplane photographs of the area to be raided.

On 27 July, Kirk and I were ordered to take out parties of all our NCOs and explore the ground over which we were to attack. We were to stay out in No Man's Land for three hours. This was really rather a stupid idea because in the actual raid we were going to make a straight charge in semi-daylight and should be able to see where we were going, so the impressions gained by crawling about in high grass in the middle of the night would not be of the slightest use to us. However, we went up to the front line at about 11.00 pm and, after hearing from the troops in the line that three enemy snipers lay out in the grass every night waiting to have a shot, we crept silently over the top and began our patrol. We did not find out anything except barbed wire and a couple of dead Tommies who must have been lying out there a very long time. We returned to our reserve dugout just before dawn after a lot of useless risk.

The date fixed for the raid was 30 July. On the 29th two cooked fowls and three bottles of whisky were sent up for us and the men also got extra rations. For some reason the date was altered to 1 August and we received another fowl and more whisky for dinner on the 31st.

August

When the day arrived we were all feeling optimistic and in good spirits. All special kit was issued in the afternoon and we got ready to move forwards. I wore my servant Butterworth's belt and bayonet, two ammunition pouches with two Mills bombs in each, and also my service revolver in its holster and my little automatic in my side pocket. The men wore fighting kit and in addition the Lewis Gun sections carried their guns and ammunition drums. Smoke bombs, wire cutters, detonator charges (for blowing up dugouts) and so on were distributed amongst the others as had been previously arranged. We went up to the front line at 8.30 pm and the men were soon spaced out and ready to start.

All raids of any size were supported by artillery, usually in the form of a 'box barrage', i.e. a barrage dropping like a curtain on three sides of the area raided so that none of the enemy within the 'box' could escape and no supporting troops could come to their assistance from outside. We had a most excellent barrage on this occasion and although I no longer remember its exact composition I believe it included the following:

2 x 9.2" howitzers – max. rate of firing 2 rounds
   per minute
4 x 6" howitzers– max. rate of firing 3 rounds
   per minute
6 x 60 pounders – max. rate of firing 4 rounds
   per minute
24 x 18 pounders– max. rate of firing 6 rounds
   per minute
36 x machine-guns – max. rate of firing 500 rounds
   per minute

In addition there were a number of 6" (Newton) and 3" (Stokes) Trench Mortars firing their powerful shells along the flanks of the attack.

Surprise is essential to success in an attack of this kind and at 9.10 pm, as the first 18 pounders cracked out from the hills behind and the shells came hissing over, we sprang up and began our dash for the sunken road. We went on steadily keeping a good line, while the air suddenly seemed alive with the shriek of shells and the earth trembled with the awful tearing crash of innumerable explosions. We were well accustomed to such shelling and a few seconds saw us safely over the enemy front line and rapidly approaching the support trenches. At this moment I saw that the men were getting too far to the right and too near the flanking barrage but, as I signalled to them to change direction a quarter left, still running forward, I tripped over the barbed wire that stretched in front of the support line and sprawled full length beyond. I was up in a couple of seconds and almost before I realized it I was standing on the edge of our objective, looking down a steep thirty-foot bank onto the road below.

I could see many dugout entrances burrowing into the ground beneath me but not a sign of life or movement. My men were perhaps twenty yards behind and, waving them forward, I slithered quickly down the bank and onto the road itself. There was still no sign of the enemy. I got out my

Mills bombs and threw the first one down some dugout steps as my men came scrambling down the bank and also began bombing the dugouts, thrusting bayonets through shelters and searching for Germans in every direction. In the meantime the Lewis gunners on the right flank had positioned their gun and thrown out some smoke bombs as a screen, but one of these dropped into the road amongst the dried-up branches of a fallen tree and rapidly set it on fire. The whole scene was strangely lit up in the gathering darkness by the glow from the flames and the flashes of the shells that continuously burst beyond us.

I was beginning to despair of capturing any prisoners when I saw a movement in the darkness down the farthest dugout to the right. I shouted down in the best German at my command that whoever was there should come out, but no one made a move though I could now discern several figures halfway down the steps. My revolver was pointed down at them and a ring of men with gleaming bayonets waited just behind me, so I suppose they were too terrified about what might happen to them if they obeyed. Then I was inspired to shout 'Kamerad, Kamerad' and they came scrambling up, chattering and gesticulating, evidently appealing to me though I did not understand a word they said. As the first one reached the top I changed my revolver into my left hand and almost reverently gripped his arm and helped him on to the road – our first prisoner!

In a minute they were all out, about a dozen of them, and Appleyard's men had just led them away to the rear when a diversion was caused by the sight of a line of men some forty yards beyond the sunken road coming straight towards us. It was getting darker now and they were extremely indistinct. A line of my men immediately ranged themselves along the forward bank and prepared to open fire, but at the last moment I thought some square objects faintly discernable on their chests looked like our familiar respirators and I gave the order not to fire. After a few moments of unpleasant uncer-

tainty I was glad I had done so. It was Kirk and his No. 2
Party who had overshot their objective, lost their way and
turned back across our front – not a very sensible proceeding.

By this time every dugout and shelter had been searched,
bombed or destroyed by demolition charges, and as there
seemed no further reason to remain I gave the order to with-
draw. Five minutes later we were all safely back in our own
front line without having sustained a single casualty. So
ended the raid, a walkover if ever there was one, though
more apparently so at the end than at the beginning. Captain
Smith and his centre party had done excellent work
capturing a machine gun and its crew in the support line as
they were on the point of setting up their gun which would
probably have wiped out my small party in the course of a
few seconds. The immediate result of the raid was twelve
Germans known to be killed (besides others who may have
been killed in the demolished dugouts) and sixteen prisoners
and one machine gun captured; but the ultimate result was
of far greater importance for it was learned from some of the
prisoners that the enemy was on the point of retreating to
the eastern bank of the River Ancre.

On the night of 2 August our Brigade occupied all the
enemy trenches west of the river and the divisions on our right
and left advanced at the same time. On 5 August the Army
and Corps commanders visited the scene of the raid and we
later received the following letter from the Army Commander:

The raid of the 10th West Yorkshire Regiment was
exceedingly satisfactory. It was well planned and
rehearsed and carried out in a determined manner. The
identifications were most valuable and the result seems
to have dislocated the enemy's preparations for retire-
ment. The battalion is to be sincerely congratulated on
its very successful enterprise.

(Signed) J Byng, General

On 5 August we were relieved by a battalion of the 38th (Welsh) Division and marched back to rest at Hérissart. We were not to enjoy our rest for very long however, for at 12 noon on 8 August entirely unexpected orders to move were suddenly received. D Company was practising platoon drill at the time and the other companies were variously engaged, but all this was stopped immediately and soon after 2.00 pm the whole Battalion was on the road. The CO (Colonel Butt) seemed to have completely lost his head on receipt of these sudden orders and marched off at the head of just one Company leaving the remainder to follow hurriedly as soon as the men could be collected. In fact some officers and men only overtook the main body by 'lorry jumping' hours after the march began. En route we heard splendid news of a successful advance that morning between Montdidier and the River Somme, and we saw long columns of German prisoners including a number of Red Cross orderlies who had been captured with a hospital train.

At 9.00 pm, after a march of 24 kilometres without any halts of more than the usual ten minutes per hour, we reached the Bois l'Abbé, a wood close to Villers-Bretonneux, in which we bivouacked for the night. We remained in this wood for the whole of the next day (9th) and after dark we marched forward to Corbie where we were billeted among the remains of the battered village. Corbie of August 1918 was very different from the Corbie of July 1916 when I had visited it last: then the buildings were sound, the shops busy and the French civilian population numerous; now many of the buildings were in ruins, the shops shut up and deserted, and the civilians gone. On the second day of our stay one of the new American battalions marched through the village and I never saw a more disreputable looking party in my life. They were a fine lot physically but their uniforms were an amazing mixture of American, French and British, and they shambled along the street out of step and out of line, with hardly a trace of discipline amongst them.

On the evening of the 12th we marched forward to relieve an Australian battalion in the front line. It was a long and rather exciting march for at about 10.00 pm we came to the attention of enemy bombing planes which continually bombed the roads hereabouts; they succeeded in causing many casualties in a C Company platoon marching a short distance from mine. At about 2.00 am we encountered some heavy shelling in the course of which my servant Butterworth was wounded and disappeared in the darkness. We were marching across open fields and as the huge shells came crashing round there was some confusion. It was not until we reached our destination half a mile further forward that I discovered that not only Butterworth, but also the Company HQ rations he had carried, were missing. We never saw the rations again, but about four months later I met Butterworth on the front at Whitley Bay nursing a badly damaged thumb.

We relieved the Australians in a country lane close to Proyart. The 'front line' was a very shallow and sketchy trench which had been hurriedly dug about seventy yards further forward. We remained there for four days during which the artillery on both sides was very active and the enemy used a great deal of gas. On the second night (13th) I took a small party forward to look for suitable shell holes for conversion into advanced machine-gun posts. I found two likely ones about sixty yards beyond the 'front line' and later the same night took out two working parties to begin the digging out. On the third night (14th) I took out a fighting patrol of twelve NCOs and men in an attempt to identify the enemy troops opposite us.

The enemy front consisted of isolated machine-gun posts at intervals, so we slipped through between two of these and reached a small post from which Very lights had been fired frequently each night. It was empty now except for used cartridges and we crept on another hundred yards to a second post from which a Very light had been fired in our direction while we were examining the first. This was also vacant now and we pushed on again a considerable distance over the high ground with the firer of Very lights always firing in front of us. Suddenly we heard whispered orders in German and my two advanced men hurried in to report that they had seen a party of about forty men moving round on the right towards our rear. At the same moment a Very light went up on our right and dropped close amongst us, blazing away in the grass within two or three feet of me. After a short interval during which we heard nothing I ordered six of my men to fire in the direction from which the Very light had come, but there was no reply except another Very light from still further towards our rear.

I began to think it was time to retire while the way was still open, so I divided my party into two of six men each and ordered one back fifty yards while I remained with the other to cover their retreat. By this means my whole party could not be rushed at once, and also I had two small groups who could fire to either flank at the same time from different points. Each time a Very light went up we fired, and after each party had passed through the other several times we got back through the enemy front line where we met a Lewis gun party under Kirk which had been sent forward on account of the firing to help to cover our return. The patrol was a complete failure so far as obtaining identification was concerned, but we did at least get out of what looked to be a most unhealthy trap; also my patrol report was quoted afterwards in Corps Intelligence as a model formation to be adopted in similar circumstances.

On the 15th Captain Smith went home on fourteen days leave and I was left in command of the Company. On the evening of the 16th we were relieved by an Australian battalion and marched back through the night to Aubigny which we reached at about 11.00 am on the 17th, after a halt for breakfast en route. We spent one night in a field under makeshift shelters of waterproof sheeting and at 10.00 pm on the following evening (18th) began a weary march to Puchevillers which we reached at 6.00 am on the 19th. The Battalion rested for the remainder of that day and on the next morning ordinary training parades began, but in the afternoon fresh orders came through stating that a new attack was commencing and that the Battalion was to move towards the line that same night (20th). Training was at once suspended and preparations for the move began, but late in the afternoon I was notified that an allotment of leave had come through and that, as I was the next officer available on the list, I was to proceed to England that night for fourteen days' leave.

I handed over the Company to Second Lieutenant Kirk, but as the last train had left Puchevillers, I watched the Battalion march off and then got a good billet in the village for the night. The following morning I caught the leave train for Boulogne and after spending one night in an hotel there, during which I slept through most of a bombing attack on the town, I crossed to Folkestone and reached Sheffield on the evening of 22 August.

So ended my active service overseas, for barely a week after my return to England I developed some form of gastro-enteritis which necessitated my remaining in bed for two or three weeks. After that a sympathetic medical board ordered me a month's convalescent treatment at Burley Hall near Oakham.

November

In due course I reported for duty once again at the Reserve Battalion HQ at Whitley Bay on 11 November, the day of the Armistice. After a dull three months at Earsden Camp, during part of which time I was Demobilization Officer, I finally demobilized myself on 8 February 1919. I received my discharge papers at Clipstone Camp and returned home to civilian life and peace after just over four years of the Army and the war.